QUEER PROFESSIONALS AND SETTLER COLONIALISM

Engaging Decolonial Thought within Organizations

Queer Professionals and Settler Colonialism works to trouble the perception of an inclusive queer community by considering the ways white lesbian, gay, bisexual, trans, and queer (LGBTQ+) people participate in larger processes and practices of white settler colonialism in Canada.

Cameron Greensmith analyses Toronto-based queer service organizations – health care, social service, and educational initiatives – whose mission and mandate attempt to serve and support all LGBTQ+ people. Considering the ways queer service organizations and their politics are tied to the nation state, Greensmith explores how, and under what conditions, non-Indigenous LGBTQ+ people participate in the sustainment of white settler colonial conditions that displace, erase, and inflict violence upon Indigenous people and people of colour regardless of their sexuality or gender identity.

Critical of the ways queer organizations deal with race and Indigeneity, *Queer Professionals and Settler Colonialism* highlights the stories of non-Indigenous LGBTQ+ service providers, including volunteers, outreach workers, healthcare professionals, social workers, and administrators who are doing important work to help, care, and heal. Their stories offer a glimpse into how service providers imagine their work, their roles, and their responsibilities. In doing so, this book considers how queer organizations may better support Indigenous people and people of colour while also working to eliminate the legacy of racism and settler colonialism in Canada.

CAMERON GREENSMITH is an associate professor in the Department of Social Work and Human Services and an affiliate faculty member in the Department of Interdisciplinary Studies at Kennesaw State University.

Queer Professionals and Settler Colonialism

Engaging Decolonial Thought within Organizations

CAMERON GREENSMITH

UNIVERSITY OF TORONTO PRESS
Toronto Buffalo London

ISBN 978-1-4875-0774-9 (cloth)   ISBN 978-1-4875-3686-2 (EPUB)
ISBN 978-1-4875-2534-7 (paper)   ISBN 978-1-4875-3685-5 (PDF)

Library and Archives Canada Cataloguing in Publication

Title: Queer professionals and settler colonialism : engaging decolonial thought within
    organizations / Cameron Greensmith.
Names: Greensmith, Cameron, author.
Description: Includes bibliographical references and index.
Identifiers: Canadiana (print) 20210352620 | Canadiana (ebook) 2021035271X |
    ISBN 9781487507749 (cloth) | ISBN 9781487525347 (paper) | ISBN 9781487536862
    (EPUB) | ISBN 9781487536855 (PDF)
Subjects: LCSH: Sexual minorities – Ontario – Toronto – Societies, etc. | LCSH: Sexual
    minorities – Services for – Ontario – Toronto. | LCSH: Settler colonialism – Ontario –
    Toronto.
Classification: LCC HQ73.3.C32 T67 2022 | DDC 306.7609713/541–dc23

We wish to acknowledge the land on which the University of Toronto Press
operates. This land is the traditional territory of the Wendat, the Anishnaabeg, the
Haudenosaunee, the Métis, and the Mississaugas of the Credit First Nation.

This book has been published with the help of a grant from the Federation for the
Humanities and Social Sciences, through the Awards to Scholarly Publications Program,
using funds provided by the Social Sciences and Humanities Research Council of
Canada.

University of Toronto Press acknowledges the financial support of the Government of
Canada, the Canada Council for the Arts, and the Ontario Arts Council, an agency of
the Government of Ontario, for its publishing activities.

**Canada Council   Conseil des Arts
for the Arts   du Canada**

**ONTARIO ARTS COUNCIL
CONSEIL DES ARTS DE L'ONTARIO**
an Ontario government agency
un organisme du gouvernement de l'Ontario

Funded by the   Financé par le
Government   gouvernement   Canadä
of Canada   du Canada

Contents

Acknowledgments

This book is a decade in the making; it emerged out of my desire – some may argue persistence – to constantly ask all sorts of questions (There is never a dumb question!). I will never forget this: I asked so many questions as a kid, my sixth-grade teacher, Mrs. Riley, would only allow me to ask a specific number of questions per day – once I hit my threshold of three, I could no longer ask questions for that day. I share this because, despite ableist past experiences, I held onto the power to question and to speak up, and, in the case of the themes in this book, engaging in relationship building, reconciliation, and decolonization continues to shape the way that I live my life, my critical orientation, and the development of this book project.

I would be remiss not to begin this book by respectfully honouring the research participants who invited me into their homes, met with me in coffee shops and bars, and trucked their way to my office at the Ontario Institute for Studies in Education (OISE) to share their stories with me – the painful and biting ones will sit with me for the rest of my life. The stories that appear within this book are only a sliver of what was shared with me. I am forever grateful for your time, energy, and commitment to social justice, antioppression, and decolonizing work. We are all lifelong learners and need one another so that we can engage in real, meaningful change that takes the roots, impacts, and effects of white settler colonialism seriously.

There are many mentors, friends, and loved ones of mine to mention here – they have made incredible and life-altering impacts on me and my thinking. The first is the quick-witted, no guff, and big-hearted husband of mine, Jeremy Tremblay. Thank you for seeing the greatness in me when I was unable to and choosing to stand by me when many would not. Your critical perspective, insight, and willingness to provide me with a different yet important perspective has made me a better scholar and had made this book the best it could be.

Second, thank you, Mike Lusiak, bad-ass writing genius and kind human. When I began this book-writing journey, I spoke to you about writing and the editorial process. Not only did you generously read, reread, and offer thoughtful criticism on my book proposal, but you also provided emotional support when I doubted myself. I cannot express enough of my thanks for you and your generosity at the beginning stages of this book-writing process.

Third, thank you, Jocelyn Sakal Froese, my writing partner and best friend; thank you for reminding me to constantly be creative and, as you put it, look sideways at what is in front of me. Your critical perspectives in comic studies, cultural studies, disability studies, and mad studies always keep me on my toes, and they informed the later iterations of the book.

Fourth, Bianca Channer, your creativity, wit, and vast knowledge base around all things social justice always keeps me excited to learn more. Getting to know you and learning with you has been one of my favourite parts of working in the Department of Social Work and Human Services at Kennesaw State University. Your gentle yet firm push and nonjudgmental approach has allowed us to cultivate a true friendship and a wonderful working relationship. Thank you for pushing me to be my best and reminding me that it is the journey that matters, not the destination.

When I arrived in academia, I began my journey as an undergraduate student in the Department of Sociology at Brock University: I had no idea what I was doing. I contemplated dropping out and thought that I was an imposter. The first class that empowered me and enabled my ongoing desire to ask questions was taught by Nancy Cook. I am so glad that I decided to take your Sexualities and Society class. Even though the class was challenging, I also found it rewarding. Thank you for using the word *partner* (instead of husband) and making space for us students who felt like misfits and outcasts in other classes. Other professors of mine who have made a long-lasting impact on me and my thinking are Kevin Gosine, Margot Francis, Jonah Butovsky, Mary-Beth Raddon, Melissa St. Germain Small, Catherine Nash, and Anna Isla. Thank you all for raising the bar high and being unapologetic in your pedagogy and teaching.

My experiences at Brock University fueled my love for research and desire to pursue graduate studies. I completed my masters in women and gender studies under the supervision of Michelle Murphy. At the time, I needed to strengthen my writing skills; while I struggled through most of my graduate work and masters research project, you constantly pushed me to be the best that I could be and fostered a safe space for me to create meaningful, rigorous, qualitative research that centred 2-Spirited people in Tkaronto/Toronto.

After completing my masters, I worked and volunteered for a year (and then some as a relief worker) at a few AIDS service organizations in Tkaronto. Throughout my work I have interacted with Black, Indigenous, and people of colour service users, service providers, and allied service providers, who shared stories with me about their frustrations with the current climate of the service sector in Tkaronto attempting to support LGBTQ2S+ peoples – what I call queer organizations. Thank you to Ann Marie Dicenso, Trevor Gray, Claudia Pabon, Bill O'Leary, Darren Nickerson, Rai Reece, Art Zoccole, and Mooky Cherian for meeting me where I was at and being patient with me as I learned the art of engaging in harm-reduction education and working closely with prisoners and exprisoners.

My experiences working within queer organizations in Tkaronto sparked my desire to pursue my doctorate. I will be forever grateful for the pieces of knowledge that I have gained and the relationships that I have built at OISE. Thank you to my supervisor, Martin Cannon, for asking the right questions and pushing me to think about my ancestry, my relationship to settler colonialism, and how best to use my voice when engaging in Indigenous-settler solidarity and research. Thank you to Scott Morgensen, committee member and postdoctoral supervisor, for pushing me to think about the relationship between white supremacy and settler colonialism, providing on-the-ground mentorship when the going was tough, and teaching me to look to history to enrich my reading of systematic violence and oppression. Thank you, June Larkin; working with you as a teaching assistant inspired me to be a student-centred pedagogue; your insights into my research project, asking me to think about the language that I use – *must*, as an example – allowed for me to see myself alongside my research participants and engage in a gentle analysis of the participants and of myself.

Others who have made monumental impacts on me and my thinking include Tanya Titchkosky, Sherene Razack, Njoki Wane, Jean Paul Restoule, Rinaldo Walcott, Alyssa Trotz, Earl Nowgesic, Jennifer Brant, Sophia Papastavrou, Adam Davies, Tara Goldstein, David Montemurro, Arlo Kempf, Juliette Hess, Leslie Stewart Rose, Carol Schick, Roland Sintos Coloma, Omisoore Dryden, Christopher Smith, Shaista Patel, Min Kaur, Percy Lezard, Hannah Dyer, Natalie Kouri-Towe, Katie Aubrecht, Eliza Chandler, Kenneth Huynh, Noah Kennealy, and Raneem Azzam.

Before landing my tenure track job at Kennesaw State University, I was a teaching assistant and adjunct faculty member at several institutions in Ontario and met wonderful colleagues and mentors, including Rebecca Raby, Shauna Pomerantz, Jeff Denis, Raven Sinclair, Chelsea Gabel, Kristin Smith, Jennifer Poole, Lisa Redgrift, Hanae Hanzawa, Gordon Pon, Alisa Craig, Nirmala Erevelles, Brenda LeFrancois, Sol Giwa, Lindsay Sheppard (who has the unfortunate job of sharing a name with someone who has a very different perspective than her), Tara Brookfield, James Cairns, Rob Kristofferson, Sue Ferguson, Victoria Tahmasebi-Birgani, Helen Fielding, and W.G. Pearson.

Kennesaw State University has been my home for five years now. I have met wonderful colleagues in different colleges and departments who have provided both emotional and scholarly support to this ambivalent Canadian now housed in Atlanta, Georgia. I am especially thankful to Mark Tillman, Scott Gordon, Susan Dyess, Leslie McClane, Neil Duchac, Michele Dipietro, Este Jordan, Minhao Dai, Sara Evans, Rodolfo Aguilar, Letizia Guglielmo, Rebecca Hill, Scott Ritchie, Jillian Ford, Ugena Whitlock, Sara Holiday, Natalia Jaramillo, LaJuan Simpson-Wilkey, Tris Utschig, and Mandy McGrew. You all have been so kind to me, have been gentle with your approach, and have provided so much insight into what being an ethical and responsible academic looks like – you all practise what you preach.

To the University of Toronto Press and specifically Meg Patterson, for believing in this book project. You have stood by the project, helped support me through the editorial process, and aided in clarifying some of my objectives. Thank you for your patience and kindness; it goes a long way in this cutthroat industry.

Finally, to Meghan Foley, for helping me refine and execute the index for this book. Thank you for your kindness, wonderful "can-do" attitude, and ongoing commitment to disability justice.

For anyone whom I have missed or forgotten, I apologize. All errors are mine, and I take full responsibility.

Thank you to all of you, from the bottom of my heart. I would not be here, wrapping up my first book project, if it was not for all your energy, time, and inspiration.

QUEER PROFESSIONALS
AND SETTLER COLONIALISM

Engaging Decolonial Thought within Organizations

Introduction: Moving beyond Acknowledging Privilege or Complicity in White Settler Colonialism

How does it come to be that the condition of modern life is Indigenous annihilation, an annihilation that so many participate in or endorse? (Razack, 2015, p. 207)

Movements for social emancipation that use claims of universal citizenship to seek full inclusion within the modern state form will do little to change the conditions by which legitimate violence continues to be naturalized as supposedly substantive attack on socially eradicable irrational practices and cultural expressions. (Reddy, 2011, p. 39)

This book explores the ways queer organizations (for- and nonprofits who centre their work around issues related to gender identity/expression and sexual orientation) in downtown Toronto can work towards meaningfully addressing ongoing oppression experienced by Indigenous peoples. I have come to this project through a series of uncomfortable accidents. Before I "came out" in my early 20s, I had been exploring the ways that my own experiences and identities were informed by encounters with cisheterosexism. Focusing on how I felt and experienced oppression – as someone who identifies as mad, queer, and a cisgender-passing person and is interpolated as part of the lesbian, gay, bisexual, transgender, queer, and 2-Spirit (LGBTQ2S+) community – allowed for me to blissfully ignore the ways I benefited from interlocking systems of oppression.

I came to this realization when I began my Master of Arts degree in women and gender studies focusing on transnational feminist thought and started working in the HIV/AIDS sector in downtown Toronto. I opted to apply to frontline opportunities (whether volunteer or for-pay) in the area of gay men's sexual health, as I wanted to grow my network, meet new people, and work closely with other "gay" men who look "like me" – white, cisgender-passing, and able-bodied – or share similar violent experiences encountering cisheterosexism. In addition to some pragmatic reasons to work with people living with and affected by HIV/AIDS, I sought to engage this work given that the field is highly saturated with gay, queer, and other men who have sex with men (MSM), assuming we shared something – anything – in common. Initially, I found applying for these jobs frustrating; most of the job applications were written with a specific skill set in mind and required professional experience (e.g., Master of Social Work, Licensed Clinical Counsellor) or with experience living with or affected by HIV/AIDS.

While chatting with one of my Indigenous colleagues about the lack of interviews I was receiving, she encouraged me to apply for an opening at another HIV/AIDS organization in downtown Toronto that worked with prisoners and ex-prisoners in Canada. At first, I shared that I did not think I was the "right person," noting that I did not have enough knowledge or experience working with that "specific population." However, as my colleague reminded me, there is a lot of overlap between the specific mandate at the organization I volunteered at and the organization that had the job opening. This invitation to think differently about my experiences and centre my investments in eradicating injustice plaguing LGBTQ2S+ peoples and communities allowed for me to see myself working within the organization and the specific service users they aim to help and support – and it did not matter if the people I was helping identified as LGBTQ2S+.

I listened to my colleague's advice, applied for the job, and was hired after what felt like an unsuccessful interview. The executive director at the time said that my experiences, as well as my training in antiracism and anticolonialism, were the reasons why I was hired – after all, Black, Indigenous, and people of colour (BIPOC) are overrepresented in the Canadian prison system (Palacios, 2016). Within this role, while not having formal training in any helping profession, I utilized my soft skills developed as a working-class youth taking part-time jobs in fast food, restaurants, hotels, and factories – my Scottish grandmother instilled in me that "if I never apply, I will never get it [the opportunity]." My working-class upbringing and experiences taught me to "roll with the punches," actively listen, and work hard (Jensen, 2012). While working at the prisoners' justice organization in Toronto and subsequent HIV/AIDS organizations working predominantly with people with concurrent disorders (e.g., who experience addiction and mental health struggles), I sought out to approach my role as a helping professional relationally by listening to the specific needs of service users and providing them appropriate harm reduction referrals (Putnam et al., 2004).

Through discussions with predominantly BIPOC ex-prisoners regarding their relationships, sex, intimacy, and drug use, as well as the daily hardships of "having a criminal record," I learned very quickly from service users themselves that HIV/AIDS organizations in Toronto were broken (Greensmith, 2015). BIPOC service users would share stories of being barred and/or banned from larger organizations (e.g., 519 Church Street Community Centre [519]) in the city of Toronto, as many of the organizations would surveil their substance use, as noted in Chapter 4. While my helping role focused on managing the drop-in space and ensuring service users had access to harm reduction education and materials, my colleagues, who were doing a lot of in-prison workshops and having conversations with prisoners on the phone, were advocating for service users' daily needs (e.g., access to antiretroviral or hormone replacement therapies) and protesting experiences of injustice in prisons across Canada. Despite this important work, I noticed that many of my colleagues were burnt out, and our relationships with other organizations in the city of Toronto seemed fractured; there was this perception that prisoners' justice work was just too radical and that the prison population were too difficult to care for and help.

Through these and other experiences, I became increasingly frustrated with the seemingly normal and mundane ways many helping professionals spoke about and worked with BIPOC – our differing experiences of oppression should be uniting us in unlearning and ultimately challenging the oppression marginalized peoples face. Evolving out of my work in Toronto's HIV/AIDS sector and subsequent interviews with 2-Spirited people attending Pride Toronto (Greensmith & Giwa, 2013) and non-Indigenous LGBTQ+ helping professionals, the goal of this book is to find a better way to engage helping – when helping itself is rooted in white settler colonial logics – and asks how non-Indigenous LGBTQ+ peoples can recognize their own (and their organizations') complicity and work towards decolonization. Decolonization, defined by Joanne Barker (2017),

> includes [Indigenous peoples'] minds and bodies in the remembrance and reform of their relations and responsibilities to the lands and ecosystems in which they live and to the other being whom they are related. This has included projects in the remembrance of their original teaching and personal accounts of their historical experiences and cultural values through multiple media of cultural production, including songs, dances, and artistry. (p. 26)

Centring Indigenous scholars', organizers', and activists' call to action of non-Indigenous peoples and larger movements in which they are involved, queer organizations in Toronto have a responsibility to meaningfully decolonize their work and engage the specific needs of BIPOC – those service users understood under the auspice of diversity, inclusion, and cultural competency – for whom queer organizations claim, and ultimately are funded, to serve.

My investment in challenging whiteness and settler colonialism within Toronto's queer communities and organizations comes from my learning about the systemic violence of whiteness globally, my white family's settler history in Canada, and my discomfort with the ways Canadian nationalism and multiculturalism erase Indigenous peoples on Turtle Island. I am forever grateful to many of my colleagues who spent extra time, energy, and care to discuss specific issues concerning BIPOC in Canada, while also reminding me that my existence (regardless of my experiences of oppression) comes to matter through my complicity; regardless of how I identify, my body is read as white, male, and cisgender-passing, and I benefit from systemic oppression. I live, breathe, and unconsciously practise white settler complicity: toxicity that surrounds my everyday life and that is fuelled through my desire to help others and appear good. Despite this investment, I remind myself that these important gifts given to me are to be used to pave a path for myself and others in positions of power to learn from our mistakes, own our privileges, and act responsibly. The premise of this book is to practise calling other white LGBTQ+ people in who have strayed away, so we can be collectively responsible for the calls to action of BIPOC academics, professionals, organizers, and activists.

Looking back on my experiences in the HIV/AIDS sector in Toronto, I was required to utilize the white logic of racial superiority – which reinforced my authoritative white gaze – to know diversity and difference. My authority, which cultivated a position through discourses of professionalism, allowed for me seemingly to determine the truth of racial difference and fold Indigeneity into race – a project of multicultural diversity, explored fully in Chapter 2. I was required to produce white LGBTQ+ peoples and communities as deserving of, and also desirable for, care and help. In my helping role, in attempting to help "the/our/my" community, I utilized white supremacist and settler colonial presumptions about and control over racial and national difference from my location as a white settler descendent. Through these experiences and my subsequent rethinking of queer organizations in Toronto, I have come to understand my role as a non-Indigenous LGBTQ+ helping professional (as well as queer organizations themselves) as sustaining and contributing to the ongoing elimination of Indigenous peoples, communities, lands, and knowledge systems (Waterfall, 2002; Wolfe, 2006).

Doing decolonial work, especially within the walls of violent organizations and helping professions, is never easy or innocent. Karyn Recollet (2013) notes that decolonization "can be perceived as an ethical way of life, whereby we [Indigenous peoples] acknowledge each other's differences and gifts and let those manifest into creating new world(s) of possibilities" (pp. 103–4). And, as Audre Lorde (1984) notes, these possibilities or futures cannot be constructed using the colonizers' or masters' tools: "they may allow us temporarily to beat him at his own game, but they will never enable us to bring about genuine change. And this fact is only threatening to those women who still define the master's house as their only source of support" (p. 98). While I want to imagine a world where social work and other helping professions are no longer necessary or required, until then, non-Indigenous professionals, regardless of their gender or sexuality, must get out of the way while simultaneously supporting antiracist and anticolonial struggles for BIPOC self-determination. This book project is an opportunity to speak back to people "like me" (non-Indigenous LGBTQ+ peoples), act responsibly towards the land that I have learned to call home (and construct my marginalized identities around), and continue to cultivate relationships beyond the bounds of gender and sexuality to uncloak the mundane – the seemingly normal – by working towards a decolonial future.

While I have illustrated my standpoint as a white settler descendant, practitioner, and scholar invested in challenging the status quo, particularly within the helping professions, the queer analysis within this book attends to historical and contemporary wrongdoings specific to Canada, with the ultimate goal of utilizing spaces of helping and healing that centre decolonization. Queer, then, can be defined as pushing against "limits within … conventions and rules, and the ways these various conventions and rules incite subversive performances, citations, and inconveniences (Britzman, 1995, p. 153). Despite queer organizations' refusal to engage the normativity of heterosexuality, they also feel pressured to adhere to missions and mandates that work to alleviate oppressions faced by service users, which are often devoid of an interlocking or systematic analysis of how oppressions experienced by gender and sexual minorities are multifaceted; oppression is often only imagined as experienced at the individual level. Thus, these organizations, such as the 519, what I call *queer organizations*, have emerged to address the deeply felt persecution gender and sexual minorities experience in contemporary Toronto, Canada. Some of these supports emerge in the form of direct one-on-one counselling addressing domestic violence in LGBTQ2S+ relationships, drop-in programs for trans and gender nonconforming peoples, harm reduction and substance use support services, as well as HIV/AIDS healthcare services.

Importantly, the existence of queer organizations demonstrates the need, on the part of public and private funders alike, to support and care for LGBTQ2S+ peoples and communities, etching queerness into the national imaginary as something to care about. As Christine Kelly (2016) notes, "care is arguably a foundational orientation and pivotal goal of many health and social science fields and policy discussions and, for many, a motivating force for the work they do" (p. 5). And this move towards caring for others can mimic the larger systems and structures of domination in Canadian society, including the reproduction of ableism and sanism. Problematic as part of a caring orientation and profession are the power and privilege caring or helping workers accrue, as they often take on a paternalistic position to help others and are placed within a relationship with someone who is receiving care (Kelly, 2016). As Leah Lakshmi Piepzna-Samarasinha (2018) notes, the cisheterosexism sedimented within care professions and organizations can often preclude (BIPOC) LGBTQ2S+ disabled folks from seeking out the care they may need: "most of us … [have] received shitty care, abusive care, care with strings attached" (p. 55).

Many of the queer organizations in the City of Toronto work towards alleviating this cisheteronormative barrier by centring LGBTQ2S+ peoples as subjects to care about. This caring ethos is also produced through public discussions on LGBTQ2S+ inclusion and diversity: stricter laws have been put in place to criminalize folks committing hate crimes, conversion therapy has been touted as an illegitimate practice and is no longer funded by the Ontario Health Insurance Plan (OHIP), and "same-but-different" politics and practices, such as same-gender marriage and adoption, are legalized and normalized. These strides have paved the way for new imaginings of how LGBTQ2S+ peoples should be cared about, what they can look like, and who they can be. While these changes have made being LGBTQ2S+ far more acceptable and normal, many marginalized LGBTQ2S+ peoples continue to be erased from queer organizations' organizing efforts (e.g., they may not be reflected in upper administration or as board members) and, when included, they exist within the lexicon of whiteness (Ahmed, 2012).

Many BIPOC activists and scholars have noted that these investments in specific imaginings of LGBTQ2S+ inclusion often go unexamined (Driskill, 2016; McCready, 2004; Muñoz, 1999; Reddy, 2011; Wilson, 1996, 2008). "Overcoming colonially imposed views of sex, sexuality, and gender, and identity is no small matter, particularly since Indigenous peoples are still experiencing colonialism in a very real way. We are not living in post-colonial times, no matter what Canadian politicians say" (Vowel, 2016, pp. 109–10). The general Canadian citizenry is encouraged to invest in white settler colonial imaginings and work towards full and total inclusion by addressing the inequality all LGBTQ2S+ people face – effectively folding Indigenous and racial difference into multicultural diversity. Yet, couched within this need to eradicate the inequality that gender and sexual minorities face remains an investment in whiteness.

This whiteness is mobilized in two separate yet linked ways. First, whiteness is made present through the sheer volume of white LGBTQ+ representation within queer organizations. For example, many of the research participants of colour whom I spoke with highlighted that the queer organizations they work within are overrepresented by white administrators, workers, and volunteers, which has the effect of over-shadowing the experiences and strengths of BIPOC peoples work-ing within these normatively white queer organizations (Greensmith, 2015). For example, Josh, a 53-year-old, queer, South Asian, cisgender man who works as a public educator at an Ontario-wide organiza-tion, stated: "look at all the programs within AIDS Service Organiza-tions. They are very much modelled after what gay white men have set out [and want]. It's like basically what they [white gay men] are saying, 'this is what everybody needs in the LGBTQ[+] [community].' The white folks set up what we need" (02/25/13, Transcript 17, p. 2, Toronto, ON). Second, the whiteness of these queer organizations man-ifests through an investment in the nation state through their fund-ing structures, which dictate how money can be spent and for whom. Funding (private and public) typically propels queer organizations into relationships with the state, and queer organizations work within these confines by creating population-specific programming and supports for all LGBTQ2S+ people in the city.

Through these examples and others, the machinery of queer orga-nizations in downtown Toronto is steeped in whiteness – a whiteness this book explores in greater detail as it has the potential to impact the ways LGBTQ2S+ activist and organizing initiatives are imagined and enacted. As Ruth Frankenberg (1993) notes, whiteness "refers to a set of cultural practices that are usually unmarked and unnamed" (p. 1). As Robin DiAngelo (2011) writes:

> Whiteness is ... conceptualized as a constellation of processes and prac-tices rather than as a discrete entity (i.e. skin colour alone). Whiteness is dynamic, relational, and operating at all times and on myriad levels.

These processes and practices include basic rights, values, beliefs, perspectives and experiences purported to be commonly shared by all but
which are only consistently afforded to white people. (p. 56)

Frankenberg (1993) and DiAngelo's work offers important interventions into the seeming naturalness of whiteness insofar as whiteness
becomes tied to a system or structure of queer organizations that often
go unexamined – reifying racial and colonial violence (Ahmed, 2012).
As noted in Chapter 2, this violence is magnified through queer organizations' desire for multiculturalism – a political and ideological force
that shapes the landscape of what it means to be Canadian. This investment in the cultures of whiteness can obscure powerful structures and
the everyday violence BIPOC routinely endure as they negotiate queer
institutions and discourses. And, within the larger arena of LGBTQ2S+
inclusion and diversity, white queerness itself can be propped up as a
mechanism of inclusion that divests energy away from antiracist and
anticolonial initiatives and activism – for who would want to change
the system they are benefiting from?

   This book addresses the specificities of queer organizations in downtown Toronto, Canada – precisely the ways queer professions, in fields
such as healthcare, counselling, and social work, address (or do not
address) the intersecting oppressions facing LGBTQ2S+ people, families, and communities. More importantly, this book highlights the need
to connect queer organizations to larger structures of oppression such
as white supremacy and settler colonialism which they routinely sustain and benefit from. White supremacy can be defined as a system of
race-based preferences that remain deeply ingrained within contemporary North America (hooks, 2003; DiAngelo, 2018; Razack, 1998, 2008;
Thobani, 2007). Indeed, as DiAngelo (2018) notes "white supremacy
[is used] to describe a sociopolitical economic system of domination
based on racial categories that benefit those defined and perceived as
white" (p. 30).

   Vowel (2016) defines settler colonialism as the "deliberate physical occupation of land as a method of asserting ownership over land and resources"
(p. 16). Moreover, settler colonialism is "predicated upon discourses of
[I]ndigenous displacement" (Byrd, 2011, p. xvii) and is an "ongoing ide-
ology and practice" (Lowman & Barker, 2015, p. 35). Like whiteness,
settler colonialism is an insidious and often taken-for-granted way of
organizing social life, which undoubtedly seeps into queer organizations
and other helping work. This book addresses an important nuance: how
do non-Indigenous LGBTQ-identified helping professionals work with
and support Indigenous peoples, communities, and nations? And how

does their helping and caring work fit within an organizational structure that is built upon Indigenous peoples' displacement, containment, and erasure?

It is undeniable that these queer organizations in Toronto do important work; that is not being questioned and will not become the central focus of this book. What is at stake here are the ways that white settler colonialism, as a logic bound up in non-Indigenous helping professionals' work and their respective queer organizations, shapes the ways queer helping work is imagined and enacted. Thus, what will be explored in more detail throughout this book are the ways white settler colonialism remains engrained in non-Indigenous LGBTQ+ helping professionals' direct practice work with marginalized service users, the mission and mandate of queer organizations, and larger outreach efforts that naturalize the whiteness of queerness while making people of colour and Indigenous people abject – as problems and pathological (Greensmith, 2012). Indeed, this book is critical of the ways queer organizations deal with race and Indigeneity by highlighting the stories of non-Indigenous LGBTQ-identified helping professionals; they are volunteers, outreach workers, healthcare professionals, clinical social workers, and nonprofit administrators who are doing the important helping, caring, and healing work. Their stories offer a glimpse into how non-Indigenous LGBTQ+ helping professionals imagine their work, their roles, and their responsibilities and considers how queer organizations may better support Indigenous peoples and participate in decolonial coalition-building that works towards eliminating white racism and settler colonialism in Canada.

Recognizing White Settler Colonialism in Canadian Institutions and Organizations

This book utilizes Sherene Razack's (2002) understanding of an unmapping as the concept brings much-needed attention to how European settlement has been naturalized. Razack illustrates that an unmapping intentionally "undermine[s] the idea of white settler innocence (the notion that European settlers merely settled and developed the land) [in order] to uncover the ideologies and practices of conquest and domination" (p. 5). As I argue throughout this book, those who claim and invest in Canadian identity must conceptualize that the foundation their identity rests upon the land, which has been produced to be terra nullius – vacant and uninhabited (Amadahy & Lawrence, 2009; Cannon & Sunseri, 2018; Pateman, 2007; Razack, 2002). The historical, social, and legal processes that have made Canada into what it is today must be unmapped to make visible the settler colonial violence that goes otherwise unseen and to connect such violent processes to the organization of contemporary social life and the queer organizations examined therein.

To give an example of one violent, and invisible, historical process of colonization, when early European settlers travelled to Mi'kmaq territory in the 1640s, they offered blankets to the Mi'kmaw people and other Indigenous peoples across Canada to unleash settler colonial consequences through biological warfare – smallpox disease (Lawrence, 2002; Ranlet, 2000). Bonita Lawrence (2002) maps out the genocide that occurred in the early contact between settlers and Mi'kmaq in Eastern Canada through the gifts of (smallpox) blankets and writes: "All of these processes were part and parcel of the colonial strategies to assert and formalize European presence and authority on the land" (p. 31). These gifts of illness acted as technologies of genocide and biological warfare that ultimately eliminated half of the Indigenous population – many of whom were Indigenous youth and elders (Lawrence, 2002). The legacy of genocide through biological means remains a current and steady force in Indigenous nations across Turtle Island: in 2009 with H1N1 swine flu and beginning in 2020 with COVID-19, "Indigenous peoples were sent body bags instead of health-care resources" (Brant, 2020, n.p.). It is clear that white settler colonialism is alive in Indigenous peoples' lives generally and is also experienced with the advent of the modern nation state and implementation of the Indian Act – a settler colonial legal system used to govern Indigenous peoples, communities, and nations across what is now called Canada.

The Indian Act, created in 1876, is a paternalistic project used to place settler beliefs and mores onto Indigenous peoples and knowledge systems to control and contain Indigenous life (Vowel, 2016). As Margot Francis (2011) argued, the Indian Act "provided a coercive and patriarchal set of cradle-to-grave directives governing Indigenous culture" (p. 10). The Indian Act placed settler colonial directives onto Indigenous communities while also inserting heteropatriarchy in Indigenous communities (Cannon, 1998; Green, 2001; Vowel, 2016). "Generations of women and their children were denied their identities and even their homes. The impact of the loss of legal identity is still being felt among Indigenous peoples through the struggle to reconnect with their families and communities" (Vowel, 2016, p. 112). While the Indian Act created particular settler colonial and cisheteropatriarchal dynamics within Indigenous and non-Indigenous communities alike, it also legislated the complete and utter removal of Indigenous children from their families through the intrusive methods of residential schooling and the child welfare system's "60s Scoop." These settler colonial regimes sought to control, contain, and erase Indigenous peoples by attacking the centre of the community: children (Anderson, 2000).

Within the context of residential schooling, white settler missionaries forcibly removed Indigenous children from their families and homes to provide them with "civilizing" education (Haig-Brown, 2009; Miller, 1996; Regan, 2010; Waterfall, 2002; Woolford, 2013; Wotherspoon, 2009; Talaga, 2017). The violent consequences of residential schooling caused Indigenous children to experience horrific cultural genocide and trauma, which continues to have long-lasting, multigenerational effects. The violence legislated within residential schooling, with the last school closure in 1996, has shape-shifted into the child welfare system to control, regulate, and repudiate Indigenous children, (grand-)mothers, and families. In particular, the infamous legislated "60s Scoop" gave white settler social workers the infinite capacity to remove Indigenous children from their families for their "best interests" (Strega & Esquao [Carriere], 2009; Pon et al., 2011; Thobani, 2007; Waterfall, 2002). As a result of such historical wrongdoings, neither helping organizations nor helping professionals are innocent in regard to their connections to reproducing, maintaining, and normalizing colonialism (Jeffery, 2009; Heron, 2007; Waterfall, 2002). Moreover, the child welfare system continues to disproportionally impact Black and Indigenous families due to the historical legacies of white supremacy and settler colonialism that continue to inform the present day (Barker, 2015; Clarke, 2010; Pon et al., 2011). Within contemporary organizations, Indigenous peoples become constructed as "problems" or "pathological" cast to the realm of the individual: a problem of their own doing (Greensmith, 2012). Yet, as Million (2013) argued, constructing Indigenous peoples' trauma as individual erases the historical, multigenerational effects of colonialism.

Indigenous communities continue to feel the weight of contemporary white settler colonialism in their lives. This gendered and sexual violence is uniquely felt by Indigenous women, girls, and LGBTQ+/2-Spirited people (Anderson et al., 2018; Hargreaves, 2017; Lavell-Harvard & Brant, 2016; Razack, 2002; Vowel, 2016). In 2004, Amnesty International released *Stolen Sisters: A Human Rights Response to Discrimination and Violence against Indigenous Women in Canada* documenting the grotesque number of Indigenous women and girls who have been murdered as well as experienced insidious gendered and sexual violence. D. Memee Lavell-Harvard and Jennifer Brant (2016) note that, despite this report being available to the public, since 2004 murders of Indigenous women and girls have continued to rise: "Indigenous women are eight times more likely to die as a result of violence, the most recent RCMP report documents 1,181 missing or murdered [Indigenous] women and girls between 1980 and 2012" (p. 2). While the conservative government under Prime Minister Harper dismissed the severity of the issue, when Prime Mister Trudeau was elected on December 8, 2015, the liberal government sought to right the historical wrongs by creating a task force to address the ways gendered and sexual violence are inflicted upon Indigenous women, girls, and LGBTQ+/2-Spirited people at alarming rates (Belcourt, 2018). While the liberal government under Trudeau sought out guidance from Indigenous families, communities, advocacy groups, and organizations, the inquiry seemed to pause on the action the Canadian government could take: "So many. Too many. So many missing. Too many gone" (Belcourt, 2018, p. xv).

As Belcourt (2018) notes, "until this country is willing to stare itself in the mirror and look to itself as the underlying reason why our sisters make up 25 percent of all cases of homicide when we are only 4 percent of the population, only then will we have taken the first step toward fixing anything" (p. xv). Indigenous feminists and activists have documented the relationship gendered and sexual violence have to settler colonialism and have outlined the historical neglect of the Canadian government in addressing persistent and longstanding genocide among Indigenous women, girls, and LGBTQ2S+ people. In 2019, *Reclaiming Power and Place: The Final Report of the National Inquiry into Missing and Murdered Indigenous Women and Girls* was released, outlining that Indigenous communities continue to experience "race, identity, and gender-based genocide" (p. 5) in addition to highlighting that the particular definitions used by Royal Canadian Mounted Police (RCMP) officials to investigate the violence Indigenous women, girls, and LGBTQ2S+ people are both "narrow and incomplete" (p. 248).

In addition to persistent violence facing Indigenous women, girls, and LGBTQ2S+ people, contemporary Indigenous life remains saturated within and constrained by the historical legacies of colonialism. The Truth and Reconciliation Commission (TRC) came into fruition in 2006 as a way for numerous non-Indigenous and Indigenous stakeholders to address the long-lasting violence and impacts that residential schools have had on Indigenous communities (Million, 2013; Regan, 2010). Most of this recognition operated through the law, in particular the *Indian Residential Schools Settlement Agreement* of 2007, wherein Indigenous peoples were asked to voice their concerns in the form of "truth telling" and share how the violence they experienced in residential schooling remained present in their everyday lives for reparations to take place (Million, 2013; Regan, 2010). Indigenous peoples were then provided with monetary compensation, specifically those who had experienced sexual or physical violence when attending residential school (Million, 2013; Regan, 2010; Simon, 2013). Although this was a step in the right direction in acknowledging the historical violence Indigenous peoples have experienced in Canada, the process further required Indigenous people to name and otherwise reveal the violence they have experienced.

As Dian Million (2013) has argued, when Indigenous peoples have to retell their stories within such TRC proceedings, they have to speak of the perpetual settler colonial trauma they and their communities have and continue to experience. However, their stories of historical and contemporary colonial violence are either reduced to an individual experience or are not heard altogether. As a result of the individualization of the colonial trauma Indigenous peoples experienced in the aftermath of residential schooling and through other settler colonial institutions, I invite non-Indigenous peoples to remember and be accountable to historical and contemporary wrongdoings that continue to constrain Indigenous life. In service of this measure, I connect Roger Simon's (2005) pedagogy of remembrance to the TRC proceedings and contemporary forms of white settler colonialism as a way to account for the divergent historical memories we all have, each with "a distinct pedagogical and political character" (p. 16). As Simon contends, a pedagogy of remembrance allows for a rereading of history, to destabilize how specific knowledge claims – which are often Eurocentric and cisheteropatriarchical – have come to be known as and produced to be legitimate and normative. As Simon quite rightly claims, "knowledge of the past is important because it can make a difference in the present" (p. 16). Non-Indigenous peoples in Canada must listen to Indigenous peoples while simultaneously acknowledging how their everyday existence manifests to offset, evict, and displace Indigenous peoples from their lands and to add to their everyday experiences of routine and relentless white settler colonial violence.

The effects of white settler colonialism remain embedded within contemporary life. If the goal of white settler colonialism is to replace and erase, what Scott Morgensen (2012) calls *emplacement*, then a haunting brings these violent, abusive, and deadly systems of power into the present day. For Morgensen, settler emplacement refers to ways in which belonging to place (e.g., the land) evolves out of social processes. If settler emplacement ensures that Indigenous erasure remains naturalized, the land and constructions of belonging to the land will remain within the non-Indigenous consciousness. Francis (2011) took up the ramifications of a collective forgetting within the non-Indigenous consciousness and argued that it cannot simply be understood as a "loss of memory"; rather, the fissures present within contemporary national imaginaries of non-Indigenous Canadians "functions as [a] haunting" and as an "affective process through which the ghosts of memory adhere within ... popular consciousness" (p. 11). The strategic deployment of historical amnesia impacts contemporary life and places Indigenous peoples as spectres of the past – constructed to be "people of a make-believe world" (Dion, 2009, p. 5), or as "noble savage[s]" (Francis, 2011, p. 11). Non-Indigenous peoples are haunted by the legacy of white settler colonialism within their everyday lives and thus need to enact a pedagogy of remembrance that works within "memory and forgetfulness to address the continuing traumas of nation building" (Francis, 2011, p. 21). Moreover, Canadian nationalism must be effectively decolonized to address the longstanding and relentless dispossession of Indigenous peoples and their lands. Otherwise, our strategic deployment of a white settler imaginary will continue to further naturalize and secure the future for white settlers at the expense of Indigenous peoples, since "emplacement on occupied indigenous lands [makes] their [white settlers'] presence seem inevitable and incontestable" (Morgensen, 2012, p. 127).

Donna Jeffery (2009) has traced the historical connection between helping work and the violent impositions of colonialism in the lives of Indigenous peoples within normative social work contexts. Although social work and other helping professions generally have been highly criticized for their deep ties to white supremacy and settler colonialism both within historical and contemporary contexts (see: Pon et al., 2011), queer organizations still receive little scrutiny in the realm of how they may sustain white settler colonialism. It is important then to consider how contemporary queerness collides with white settler colonialism (Hunt & Holmes, 2015; McNeil-Seymour, 2015). Although the inception of queer organizations occurred in conjunction with the civil rights movement, queerness as a modern project is deeply rooted in white settler colonialism. As Morgensen (2011b) argues, "queers within a white settler state ... become modern through homonationalist participation in colonial and imperial rule that awards citizenship for defending the state and educating subject peoples in civilizational values, including sexual modernity" (p. 226). As a result, the foundation queer organizations rests upon white settler professionals have invested in the Canadian nation state and the settlement process. To justify their pretence of global "community," and to appeal to state multiculturalism, queer organizations fold people of colour into projects that still reproduce white settler colonial power relations to Indigenous peoples and their lands. Building upon Canada's white settler colonial foundation, queer organizations came to fruition and evolved to fill a critical gap and support LGBTQ2S+ people who were experiencing violence and oppression due to their sexual minority status and gender identity/ expression.

Beyond Acknowledging or Naming One's Privilege

To address the complexities of queer organizations and the action (and inaction) of non-Indigenous LGBTQ+ helping professionals, I connect their work within the larger scholarship of privilege and complicity. I do so to unravel and unearth – unsettle – the ways whiteness and settler colonialism latch onto queerness to erase, inflict violence upon, and abjectly mark BIPOC – to effectively reproduce queerness as property of whiteness (Muñoz, 1999). Privilege as a concept has become part of helping professionals' vernacular, offering them – many of whom are privileged subjects – an opportunity to reconsider how they might connect their biographies to larger systems and structures of inequality.

Peggy McIntosh (2010) introduced the concept of *white privilege* through the metaphor of an invisible backpack: privileged people carry their privileges with them even if they might not ever recognize their impact and effect on them and the individuals they interact with. For example, as part of MacIntosh's conscious-raising tactic, she offers a checklist for privileged subjects to soak in how they benefit from the larger societal structure: "2. I can avoid spending time with people whom I was trained to mistrust and who have learned to mistrust my kind of me; 5. I can go shopping alone most of the time, pretty well assured that I will not be followed or harassed" (p. 16). While MacIntosh's work has set the foundation for how to begin a dialogue around white-male and other forms of privilege, her work has the potential to dilute the complex structural and intersecting realities powerful subjects live within and contribute to. Adding complexity to privilege discourse and dialogue, Devon Carbado (2005) addresses the complexities of privilege through an intersectional lens, noting: "A white heterosexual man lives in the white side of race, the male side of gender, and the straight side of sexual orientation. He is, in this sense, the norm. Mankind. The baseline. He is our reference. We are all defined with him in mind. We are the same as or different from him" (p. 192). Here, Carbado pushes theories of privilege beyond the individual's lexicon and suggests that the concept must be connected to the larger social and cultural arena – highlighting how privilege and power intersect to create what Carbado calls *the baseline* or *mankind*.

Carbado's analysis of privilege, while helpful, is often disregarded in the helping professions. Instead, helping professionals are asked to consider how their privileges can be effectively understood under the auspice of "cultural competency" and effectively used in their helping roles – as a mechanism to aid in developing and sustaining a helping relationship. Within cultural competency or diversity training, the complex analysis of privilege often goes unaddressed, locating such a discussion in the realm of the individual – disconnected from larger systems and structures of inequality (Schick & McNinch, 2009). Helping professionals are routinely encouraged to "develop sensitivity toward, appreciation for, understanding of and knowledge about 'the other'" (p. xiii). Yet, disconnected from this understanding of difference, or "otherness," is a full and complete analysis of how power and privilege play out – especially within helping relationships. And, when privilege is engaged through such pedagogical practices, the perception that one needs to name or confess one's privileges rises to the forefront (Lensmire et al., 2013).

This act of confession is encouraged; as Ann Bishop (2002) notes, "count your privileges; keep a list. Help others see them. Break the invisibility of privilege" (p. 116). Yet all of this work surrounding privilege fuels helping professionals' seeming goodness and perception that they are not *part of* the problem; that is, this work to know, understand, and name one's privilege often does not address the structural inequalities persistent within helping relationships and professions generally. And those who appear good often find themselves within the helping professions; as Carol Schick and Verna St. Denis (2005) note: "helping others is proof of one's privileged positioning" (p. 308). Having the opportunity to help is indeed a privilege in itself and can be used as a form of cultural capital that can alienate helping professionals from the communities in which they want to help. Thus, focusing on *only* privilege may not provide helping professionals with a full picture of oppressions that exist within contemporary Canadian society and the helping professions more specifically.

Despite the important relationship privilege has to larger systems of inequality, much of the ways privilege is discussed and practised within the helping professions remains within the realm of the individual: one needs to chart their privileges, name them, and in doing this they are released from the web of guilt knowing one's privileges insures. Jafri (2012) notes, "We can't simply shake off or 'check' our privilege at the door. And it's not simply about being mindful of a knapsack we're carrying. Declarations of privilege can just as easily re-inscribe dominant subject positions, by centring the focus on the unlearning process of the dominant subject" (n.p.). DiAngelo (2018), in conducting many anti-racist workshops, describes a common phrase said by whites: "'Just because of the color of my skin, I have privilege'" (p. 63). DiAngelo notes that statements regarding white privilege such as these "seem [like] a fluke – something that just happens to us [white people] as we [white people] move through life, with no involvement or complicity on our part" (p. 64). Thus, the discourse of privilege can be dangerous, as it has the potential to erase the ways individual biographies are connected to systems and structures of oppression.

To name the gaps entangled within privilege discourse, especially in how it is taken up within education and the helping professions, Barbara Applebaum (2011) suggests that privilege must connect to our understanding of complicity – as a way to name our often-unrealized connections to larger systems of inequality from which we benefit. We are not just individuals existing in the world; rather, we exist in a world that interpolates us and gives us value – unknowingly or not, we are always connected in our sameness or difference. For Applebaum, being able to name one's privilege is unhelpful in enacting real change. Instead, acknowledging, recognizing, or resisting complicity can become a call to action to realize how one benefits in the larger order of things and act to change the situation. The key piece for Applebaum is that privileged subjects can work alongside others to form and forge alliances to unravel and work against systems of inequality. This change can have monumental effects: privileged subjects are encouraged to give up or otherwise change the system from which they benefit, making such a realization destabilizing.

DiAngelo's (2018) work on white fragility addresses ways whites effectively respond to their privilege and complicity in the form of "discomfort and anxiety," which is "born out of superiority and entitlement" (p. 2) aimed at protecting the unearned advantage. White fragility as a concept is useful insofar as it provides a space to centre the privileged white subject and the work done in order to resist dismantling white supremacy despite claims of liberalism or progress. Many privileged subjects working within the helping professions, which are typically entrenched within contemporary neoliberal logic, are able to disconnect their personal biographies from the white institutions in which they work. As Amy Rossiter (2001) argues, "we are always acting in and through a history in which the contradictions of history are lived out in our practices, and no person – even ones who do it perfectly[–] can be extracted from history" (n.p.). That is, our relationships to the helping profession are neither ambivalent nor innocent; rather, helping within the professional field, whether education or social work, has emerged from a dark history of conquest and domination (e.g., the forced removal of Indigenous children from their families to attend residential schools across Canada), and that history remains today (Linklater, 2014; Lowman & Barker, 2015; Vowel, 2016; Waterfall, 2002). And, to locate the discussion within the context of contemporary queer organizations, an intersection that is routinely removed from privilege and complicity discourses is the ways white LGBTQ+ subjects can be complicit in the oppression of "others."

While many LGBTQ2S+ people claim that they are only oppressed subjects, such a claim ignores their relationships to power and privilege – specifically white supremacy and settler colonialism. As Cathy Cohen (1997) writes, queerness is always embedded in race, class, and gendered privilege. Cohen notes that occupying the category of "queer" means to exist in a world that understands its meaning and legitimatizes it into consciousness. The legitimacy situates queerness within the lexicon of whiteness whereby within the North American context the images, symbols, and language associated with queerness are wrapped up in the normativity of whiteness. Expanding on this further, Jasbir Puar (2007) argues that "queer operates as an alibi for complicity with all sorts of other identity norms, such as nation, race, class, and gender, unwittingly lured onto the ascent towards whiteness" (p. 24). The relationship queerness has to whiteness in its legibility cannot be denied, thus, claims of LGBTQ2S+ subjects' oppression can further legitimize the whiteness of queerness while simultaneously denying their complicity in existing oppressions.

And while it is important to situate LGBTQ2S+ subjects in transnational networks of privilege and oppression, it is equally important to expand upon such an analysis to include whiteness and settler colonialism. As such, Scott Morgensen's (2011a, b, c) important work on queer settler colonialism situates the above analysis of white queer formations within the larger arena of Indigenous erasure in the Americas. Morgensen contends that non-Indigenous LGBTQ+ peoples should "question the colonial origins and use of sexual minority and queer identities, displace desires for a history or future on stolen land, and challenge the colonial power of settler states and global institutions" (p. 134). This move towards a conscious awareness of white settler colonialism calls in non-Indigenous LGBTQ+ folks to take seriously the settler colonial conditions that make their lives, experiences, and identities legitimate and liveable, asking how such livability is predicated on the erasure, displacement, and abjection of Indigenous peoples.

Indeed, understanding the imbricated logics of queerness, whiteness, and settler colonialism aids in understanding how seemingly innocent

evocations of LGBTQ2S+ inclusion, rights, and diversity perpetuate and sustain inequality, rather than eradicate it. Working towards
new thought and action within queer activism, communities and organizations must challenge the ways white queerness can erase BIPOC
(LGBTQ2S+ or not). This is especially important since queer organizations in their structure attempt to work in solidarity with BIPOC; thus,
attending to the ways queer organizations were formed and how they
have changed is especially important if such decolonial praxis is to be
developed and sustained. Indeed, directing attention towards the work
of queer organizations offers important insight into the practices of
exclusion occurring and the potentiality for a new simultaneously. In its
entirety, this book theorizes the extent to which white settler colonialism
is naturalized in queer communities and thus also within queer organizations in downtown Toronto. Although these queer organizations are
being called progressive on the continuums of gender identity, sexuality, and desire, little attention is paid to how they can potentially contribute to and easily sustain everyday evocations of settler colonialism.

Research Study, Context, and Methods/Methodology Used

Situated within the context of downtown Toronto, this book makes use
of the in-depth one-on-one interviews of 41 non-Indigenous LGBTQ+
helping professionals working in LGBTQ2S+ organizations that aim to
serve a multitude of service users from racial, ethnic, and national origins. Throughout the book, the interview data is presented to the reader
using direct quotations or is paraphrased to centralize the research
participants' lived experience from their standpoint. Interviews were
conducted to try to understand the phenomena from participants' perspectives and to understand how they experience their social world
(Kvale & Brinkmann, 2009). All of the research participants worked in
downtown Toronto and come from numerous organizations all engaging with LGBTQ2S+ programming for their target populations. Pro-
spective research participants needed to meet the following criteria:
(1) identify as non-Indigenous and LGBTQ+; (2) work, or have worked
during the time of the interview, at a queer organization in downtown
Toronto; and (3) be over the age of 18. Participants were asked questions such as their experiences working within queer organizations and
the ways they intend to support BIPOC and to inquire as to how their
work could be strengthened, modified, or changed. I engage the stories
of the research participants using a queer analysis to make space for
new engagements and possibilities that exist "beyond or between the
normativity of representation" (Greensmith & King, 2020, p. 4).

I have chosen to seek out the stories and experiences of non-Indigenous helping professionals so as specifically not to recolonize Indigenous peoples through the research process (Absolon & Willett, 2005; Max, 2005; Smith, 1999, 2012). As Linda Tuhiwai Smith (1999) argues, "'Research' is probably one of the dirtiest words in the [I]ndigenous world's vocabulary" (p. 1). Qualitative and quantitative research have long been used as tools of imperial and colonial domination, which continually produce Indigenous peoples as objects of inquiry (Smith, 1999). By speaking to predominantly non-Indigenous research participants, this project aims to reduce and limit the white supremacist and settler colonial violence enacted on Indigenous peoples within the qualitative research-gathering process. I acknowledge that as a queer, white, settler critic of white settler colonialism I can only think through the experiences of white LGBTQ+ peoples since I will never truly be able to understand the experiences of BIPOC.

This book addresses the ways non-Indigenous LGBTQ helping professionals (29/41, or 71 per cent, of the participant sample self-identified as white, a white settler, or Caucasian) come to understand their roles and responsibilities when working with Indigenous peoples. I interview non-Indigenous peoples (mixed-race helping professionals (2/41, or 2 per cent, of the participant sample) and helping professionals of colour (10/41, or 24 per cent, of the participant sample) better to understand how queer organizations and workers in Toronto understand, imagine, and work with Indigenous peoples (see Tables 1 and 2 for participant demographics). The project thus centres the non-Indigenous subject as an object of study – given the Indigenous-led activist movements, scholarship, and public resources that call on non-Indigenous peoples to take action in addressing Indigenous genocide in Canada and globally.

Indigenous peoples were not interviewed given the project's focus on considering the investigatory relationship between non-Indigenous and LGBTQ+ identities and subjectivities within queer organizations in Toronto. This specific focus allowed me to explore the topics of whiteness and settler colonialism more openly with non-Indigenous research participants.

Audio recordings were transcribed verbatim and destroyed upon completion. Once each interview was conducted, participants were asked to choose a pseudonym to ensure confidentiality; many participants declined, and a name was chosen on their behalf. Participants were also asked to share recruitment information with others who might be interested. Also, to ensure the utmost reliability of the data, member checking was used, which involves research participants reviewing their transcript to ensure accuracy while giving them a

Table 1. Participant Demographics (Race/Ethnicity)

Race/Ethnicity	Participants
White	28
South Asian	4
Mixed-Race	2
Latino	2
Portuguese	2
White Settler	1
Mestiza	1
Asian	1

Table 2. Participant Demographics (Gender/Sexuality)

Sexuality	Response Rate
Queer	16
Gay	12
Gay/Queer	5
Lesbian	2
Bisexual/Queer	2
Genderqueer	1
Lesbian/Queer	1
Tri-Sexual	1
Dyke	1

chance to review the material and adding or deleting content as they see fit. Primary and secondary coding were used to draw out themes (Kvale & Brinkmann, 2009).

Organization of This Book

Chapter 1, "Understanding the Historical and Contemporary Realities of (White) Queer Organizations in Toronto," addresses the emergence of queer organizations as necessary interventions to existing cisheteronormative inequalities plaguing LGBTQ2S+ people – from the 1970s to the present day. This chapter also highlights the research participants' own understanding of their organizations and the queer programming occurring to support LGBTQ2S+ peoples' experiences with cisheterosexism and other forms of oppression. Chapter 2, "'We Had the Rainbow': Queer Organizations and the Desire for White Settler Multiculturalism," situates contemporary organizations within the Canadian national imaginary whereby these organizations and helping professionals alike invest in multiculturalism and diversity through their evocation of Canadian queer politics.

Chapter 3, "'People Like Me?': Non-Indigenous LGBTQ+ Professionals' Helping Motivations," traces the ways helping professionals' past experiences of oppression impact their understanding and enactment of their contemporary enactment of helping work. Here, white LGBTQ+ helping professionals evoke the understanding of "like me," which shapes who is imagined as deserving of, but more importantly receives, help. Ultimately, the helping work and imagined white LGBTQ2S+ people in need of help shape the queerness within Toronto's queer organizations. Chapter 4, "Necropolitical Care: The Practice of Indigenous Exclusion," provides an analysis of how Indigenous peoples are specifically excluded from queer organizations. This chapter contends that the structure of queer organizations and the practices of non-Indigenous LGBTQ+ helping professionals perceive Indigenous peoples as problems, pathological, or, at times, too difficult to care for and thus excludable from queer organizations.

Chapter 5, "A Call to Action: Queerness, Complicity, and Deflecting Responsibility," addresses the ways white LGBTQ+ helping professionals see themselves, their profession, and their work as contributing to the goal of diversity and inclusion. Here, non-Indigenous LGBTQ+ helping professionals articulate the various ways they (knowingly or unknowingly) deflect responsibility in working against white settler colonialism. In turn, by understanding themselves and their actions as contributing to a *common good*, non-Indigenous LGBTQ+ helping professionals remain complicit in the violent BIPOC experience. The conclusion, "Building Decolonial Alliances and Working towards Queer Coalitions across Difference," considers the ways non-Indigenous LGBTQ+ helping professionals can work towards accountable and responsible relationships with BIPOC that challenge white settler colonialism in which queer organizations and professions typically naturalize. Here, I juxtapose good intentions of non-Indigenous LGBTQ+ helping professionals with larger discussions of accountability to illustrate how all LGBTQ+ people might engage in alliances, solidarity work, and coalitions beyond the walls of their queer organization or profession. I end this chapter with a series of questions for non-Indigenous helping professionals and others interested in working towards eliminating white settler colonialism by holding themselves and their organizations responsible.

Author Note: Final Thoughts

This book is a conversation and invitation to think differently about helping professionals' habitual practices in Toronto, Canada. As a white critic of white settler colonialism, I utilize this book as a platform to hold myself accountable to the critiques of BIPOC within and outside of the helping professions. Thus, throughout this book, I must consider how BIPOC are already working together to challenge, subvert, and break down white supremacy and settler colonialism. Throughout the analysis of queer organizations in Toronto, including non-Indigenous LGBTQ+ research participants' stories, I engage an analysis of whiteness and settler colonialism whereby I differentiate between white helping professionals and non-Indigenous helping professionals respectively. Utilizing white criticism of white settler colonialism, this book challenges the whiteness of queer organizations by uplifting the queer-of-colour critiques of the LGBTQ+ research participants of colour, noting that they have a different relationship to whiteness and settler colonialism (Amadahy & Lawrence, 2009; Byrd, 2011; Cannon, 2012; Fujikane & Okamura, 2008; Jafri, 2012, 2013; King, 2015; Lawrence & Dua, 2005; Vowel, 2018).

Thus, in order to be accountable to the process and practices of white settler colonialism in which I and other white settlers participate, we should not erase Canada's genocide, anti-Black, and colonial history in the form of historical amnesia (Dion, 2009; Razack, 2002) but, instead, enact what Simon (2005) calls a *pedagogy of remembrance*. I ask that my readers fully engage with the stories shared here by the non-Indigenous LGBTQ+ research participants that challenge and/or reify white settler colonialism within queer organizations and other helping professions more broadly.

Chapter One

Understanding the Historical and Contemporary Realities of (White) Queer Organizations in Toronto

Introduction

While the analysis of this book engages queer organizations and non-Indigenous LGBTQ+ helping professionals in downtown Toronto, it is important to historicize the work done. This chapter traces out the historical moments that shifted the public consciousness surrounding LGBTQ2S+ issues and identity politics – specifically moving LGBTQ2S+ politics in Canada towards discussions of humanity and rights. These important shifts paved the way for Toronto and the rest of Canada to understand LGBTQ2S+ advocacy initiatives and organizations as part of larger processes and practices of nation-building, which is explored in Chapter 2. The services and supports for LGBTQ2S+ peoples and communities emerged as a response to the existing and persistent inequalities faced. The development of LGBTQ2S+ activist-led initiatives paved the way for contemporary queer organizations and services generally and, moreover, for the non-Indigenous LGBTQ+ helping professionals in the queer organizations to understand the work that they do as legitimate, sustainable, and worthy of public attention and funding.

This chapter, which begins engaging archival data from the 1970s, highlights key moments in queer Canadian/Ontarian contemporary history that are typically used to bolster queer organizations' and non-Indigenous LGBTQ+ helping professionals' investments in LGBTQ2S+ issues. In conjunction with the narratives of the research participants who discuss the larger arena of queer organizations and the emergence of LGBTQ+ helping in Canada. Jamie, a 24-year-old white, queer, cisgender woman who works as a volunteer at a youth organization, discussed how working within the "gay community" can have limiting consequences. As she stated: "When I am living my everyday life, I am surrounded by so much queer stuff. Working in the gay community and all of my other work, sometimes I forget what reality is or what other lives are like and how impactful it is" (03/27/13, Transcript 32, p. 4, Toronto, ON). Jamie discussed with me how her queer life and the explicit gay focus of her work can sometimes inhibit her perception of reality and limit her capacity to truly understand other queer peoples' experiences of oppression. Although Jamie is working within the "gay community," she talked about how LGBTQ2S+ people should not stop challenging cisheterosexism and homophobia even though same-gender marriage is now legalized. To further her point, Jamie brought up two examples of LGBTQ2S+ teen suicide and cases of international homophobia as necessary causes to support. Jamie's story, which is echoed by many of the research participants, notes that there is a need and desire for queer organizations. As discussed later, queer organizations emerged in downtown Toronto as a way to support and advocate for the LGBTQ2S+ community by providing frontline supports and services.

Historicizing Queer Organizations

Within the North American context, the "beginning" of activism and social change for LGBTQ2S+ peoples is often evoked in the Stonewall riots in June of 1969 (Arriola, 1995). For three days, gay men, lesbians, and trans people fought back against police surveillance and violence at a local gay bar in Greenwich Village in New York City. "Deviant" patrons, such as drag queens and butch lesbians, were "arrested and taken away in a paddy wagon, while white, male customers looked on or quietly disappeared" (Matzner, 2015, p. 2). These riots effectively brought lesbian, gay, and trans identities and issues into public consciousness and out of the proverbial closet. Erased from narratives surrounding the Stonewall riots are the trans women of colour such as Marsha P. Johnson and Sylvia Rivera who utilized their anger in their advocacy and activist efforts to bring awareness to the violence targeting gay men, lesbians, and trans people. Importantly, the Stonewall riots highlighted the persistence of gay men, lesbians, and trans people in challenging police violence towards LGBTQ2S+ peoples and opened up the conversation surrounding sexual liberation and freedom.

Alongside important advocacy and activist initiatives in the United States, in 1973 the international American Psychiatric Association's *Diagnostic and Statistic Manual of Mental Disorders* (DSM) removed homosexuality as a mental illness (Drescher, 2015). The removal of homosexuality from the DSM was an important intervention in the medical and psychiatric treatment of gay men and lesbians, as their desires and sexual acts could no longer be controlled and contained by a pathological diagnosis. For example, once diagnosed as a homosexual, gay men and lesbians would often undergo electroshock therapy or castration, since medical officials could not find a cure to this "problem" (Milar, 2011). Within the Canadian context, noted in The Body Politic[1] (1972), this change in the DSM effectively made homosexuality legal, which allowed activists to argue that the Ontario Human Rights Code (OHRC) should include sexual orientation by protecting "gay civil liberties." In 1973, homosexuality was advocated for as a protected identity category in Ontario, and this activism paved the way for larger discussions of LGBTQ2S+ inclusion and, more importantly, the fact that *homosexuals* could no longer experience inhuman treatment, torture, or discrimination as people.

Importantly, the removal of homosexuality from the DSM in the context of queer organizing must be understood as an opportunity insofar as homosexuals (who are now called *gays* and *lesbians*) were granted humanity through an internationally recognized and powerful body of experts, the publication of which is still used today by psychiatrists, social workers, and other helping professionals. However, it is important to note that, while gays and lesbians still experience strife and inequality, the understanding that they are human (no longer considered deranged or pathological) paved the way for a larger cultural shift, one that gays and lesbians themselves utilized to address the prevailing inequality and oppression experienced. As a result, in 1973, the Hassle Free Clinic (formally the Roachdale Free Clinic) emerged shortly thereafter to advocate for the health needs of gay men, lesbians, and trans people who were being underserved by healthcare professionals or denied services all together. The Hassle Free Clinic is a "community-based clinic [that provides] medical counselling services in all areas of sexual health" (Hassle Free Clinic).

Moreover, due to the increase of sexually transmitted diseases (STDs), now called sexually transmitted infections (STIs), among gay men, lesbians, and trans people as public-health-designated "risk groups," the Hassle Free Clinic started to offer anonymous testing, even though it was illegal at the time. The clinic remains an important service for marginalized and underserved LGBTQ2S+ peoples and is known publicly as a safe and nonjudgmental space surrounding all things (queer) sexual health. In addition to healthcare services for LGBTQ2S+ peoples, more community-wide advocacy initiatives and supports emerged as opportunities to create and cultivate a unified community. In 1975, 519 emerged as a community space for LGBTQ2S advocacy; the organization has grown substantially to address the "inclusion, acceptance, and awareness of LGBTQ2S rights in Toronto and beyond" (519 Church Street Community Centre). The 519 emerged as a community organization to address the longstanding injustice facing LGBTQ2S+ peoples and to provide spaces for community members to organize.

The 519 has gained immense popularity for its being situated in Toronto's "gay village" but also its investment in fostering and creating community. As Mark Casey (2004) contended, the "gay village" typically "belongs to the non-heterosexual population of the city, sharing similar social and leisure spaces, shared friends, experience, values and so on" (p. 449). Christina Hanhardt (2013) theorized the Greenwich Village in New York City and argued that the very project of the "gay village" and of "community" rests upon gendered, raced, and classed inequality. Therefore, whereas at first glance Toronto's gay village might be representative of a collective community, one that is produced through 519 programming, in actuality it is white, gay, cisgender men with financial capital who ultimately have decision-making power surrounding the direction of "the community" and subsequent queer organizations in Toronto's downtown core, as noted by Josh in the introduction.

While Toronto's "gay village" offered spaces for social cohesion and activism, gays and lesbians continued to be highly surveilled by the police (Nash, 2005, 2006). In 1981, bathhouse raids occurred whereby the police infiltrated four of Toronto's bathhouses and charged "204 men as 'found-ins' and 20 others as 'bawdy house keepers'" (Nash & Bain, 2007, p. 163). The bathhouse raids provide a context to illustrate how the "gay male community" gathered together in response to the police brutality inflicted upon them, similar to the Stonewall riots. The raids also produce a popular understanding among gays, lesbians, and trans people that they are continually to face violence at the hands of the police and other public officials. Toronto gay activist Tim McCaskell organized a meeting at 519 that hundreds of people attended to spontaneously protest the police and illustrate that public sex and queer affection could no longer be understood as illegal and abnormal (Nash & Bain, 2007), even when *homosexuality* was removed from the DSM. This activist and organizing initiative started as the annual Pride march – now housed under the not-for-profit Pride Toronto, which has received a lot of scrutiny for operating under capitalism (Greensmith & Giwa, 2012) and, as discussed in Chapter 2, criticized for reinforcing anti-Black and anti-Native racism. In addition to activist endeavours addressing police brutality and the target of gays, lesbians, and trans people in the early 1980s, HIV/AIDS activism occurred due to the HIV virus impacting, affecting, and brutally killing gay men, injection-drug users, and sex workers in North America and globally (Cain, 2002; Rayside & Lundquist, 1992).

In the early 1980s, people living with and affected by HIV/AIDS gathered together in response to the HIV/AIDS epidemic in Canada and formed AIDS Service Organizations (ASOs). Toronto's first ASO, the AIDS Committee of Toronto (ACT), formed in 1983 to assist those affected by HIV/AIDS, to provide support for those who had lost a friend, relative, or lover to the virus, and to educate one another on the virus and other STIs (Rayside & Lundquist, 1992). The ACT works to "reduce new HIV infections in Toronto and promotes the independence, dignity, health and well-being of people living with HIV and AIDS" (AIDS Committee of Toronto, 2016). While the HIV/AIDS epidemic drastically and negatively impacted LGBTQ2S+ communities, it also brought many disparate communities together to advocate for pharmaceuticals, for direct care for those who were dying, and for community supports such as meals, transportation to medical appointments, and in-home support. Soon after the immense work of LGBTQ2S+ and allied community activists and organizers, on May 6, 1986, "the Ontario government committee votes to include in its package of proposals to the Ontario legislature the amendment of the Ontario Human Rights Code to include sexual orientation protection" (Rites, 1986). For gays and lesbians living in Ontario, this legislative change allowed for cases of discrimination with regard to sexual orientation to be taken seriously at the provincial level – creating a culture that legitimized (through the province) particular forms of gay and lesbian identity.

With this monumental shift in Ontario's political climate and the death rate for those impacted and affected by HIV/AIDS climbing due to unsustainable treatment options, in 1988 Casey House emerged as a respite healthcare facility and primary care unit for people living with AIDS: "With an innovative and interprofessional approach to healthcare, we empower the lives of people living with HIV/AIDS. We believe in the importance of client-driven care achieved through deliberate inclusivity, unequivocal compassion, and mindful collaboration" (Casey House, 2021). It is clear that during the 80s and beyond, HIV/AIDS became the centre of many LGBTQ2S+ activist and advocacy efforts, and as a result many queer organizations today evolve out of existing and longstanding HIV/AIDS organizations that mark Toronto as a queer-friendly and supportive place for LGBTQ2S+ peoples.

In the 90s, more queer organizations started to emerge to meet the different needs of LGBTQ2S+ community members. For example, in 1992, Teens Educating and Confronting Homophobia (TEACH), part of Planned Parenthood, appeared to address the prevailing inequality LGBTQ2S+ and questioning youth experience and also to engage in educational workshops and programming for the general public (Planned Parenthood). In 1998 two organizations were formed: Supporting Our Youth (SOY), a drop-in after-school program for LGBTQ+ and questioning youth as part of the Sherbourne Health Centre, and also the LGBTQ2S-specific addictions-support program Rainbow Services was introduced by the Centre for Addiction and Mental Health to address persistent and prevailing addictions typically used as a mechanism to cope with everyday forms of cisheterosexism (Centre for Addiction and Mental Health, 2021). Importantly, with new changes towards how to mobilize and engage in LGBTQ2S+ advocacy, under the auspice of these larger, well-funded queer organizations LGBTQ2S+ peoples and their allies gained the opportunity to keep up the momentum to alleviate the persistent and longstanding inequality experienced. Also, queer organizations can apply for and be awarded public and private funding (local, provincial, national, and international) to address behavioural, social, and cultural concerns impacting and affecting LGBTQ2S+ peoples and communities in Toronto. From the 2000s and onward, many organizations emerged, including the Sherbourne Health Centre, which is one of the most widely used healthcare facilities for transgender and gender-nonconforming people in Toronto/Ontario, illustrating how these historical moments provided the space for queer organizations (both for-profit and nonprofit) to understand that LGBTQ2S+ peoples are generally worthy of care and help and that their experiences of oppression and inequality are worth mitigating.

Thinking about Contemporary Queer Organizations

Discussing the historical emergences of queer organizations and their mission statements alongside important cultural moments surrounding gays, lesbians, and trans people sets the tone for what kind of advocacy or direct practice work is made to be possible. For example, gay, lesbian, bisexual, and trans people's rights are protected under the Ontario Human Rights Code. Cain (2002) describes queer organizations (of which many are ASOs) as "community-based organizations, often explicitly grounded in the belief that community mobilization, personal and collective empowerment, self-help, and helping each other are crucial elements in the fight against HIV" (p. 94). Importantly, the research participants' narratives offer a different entry point from their own lived experiences into understanding the purpose of contemporary queer organizations in Toronto. Many of the white, cisgender, male research participants expressed that one of the main reasons queer organizations in Toronto exist is to combat and fight against the HIV/AIDS virus (see: Rayside & Lundquist, 1992), given that MSM accounts for 60 per cent of new diagnoses in Ontario (Ontario HIV Treatment Network, n.d.). John, a 54-year-old gay, white, cisgender man, discusses with me why the work he does is important and notes "the first people that were contracting HIV in Toronto were largely gay men" (03/21/13, Transcript 30, p. 4, Toronto, ON).

The focus of HIV/AIDS and STI prevention and education is produced through queer organizations' investments in acquiring funding to aid in supporting the development of individuals and reducing risk. For example, many organizations adopt public-health language, such as *MSM*, to account for service-user behaviour (e.g., using pre-exposure prophylaxis [PrEP] or not using a condom when having anal or oral sex), rather than placing the focus on the social and cultural factors that impact one's health (see Young & Meyer, 2005). Helping professionals are encouraged to implement public-health interventions in their practice as well as interact with service users by adopting the judgment-free language. In framing service users through their behaviour, helping professionals can easily individualize the experiences of service users, which requires them to disengage with how racism and colonialism become social determinants of health (Czyzewski, 2011; Giwa & Greensmith, 2012).

Although HIV/AIDS and behaviour of gay, cisgender men and other MSM can become centralized within queer organizations due to their perceived sexual or behavioural health risk, Brandon, a 53-year-old gay, white, cisgender man who works as a community-based researcher at a large ASO, provided a different perspective: "we need gay men services for gay men by gay men ... it is really sad that there are none in the city" (03/09/13, Transcript 22, p. 7, Toronto, ON). From Brandon's standpoint, queer organizations in Toronto, even if they focus on HIV/AIDS, do not explicitly address the needs of or centre gay men. Contrary to Brandon's experience, many research participants, including Josh in the introduction, have noted that gay experience is privileged, and their experiences seem to be given more attention (even if not named under the banner of "gay services"). Centralizing "gay" within queer organizations' programming and services can easily erase many LGBTQS2+ BIPOC who cannot be easily captured under the banner of "gay" (Driskill et al., 2011; Gopinath, 2005; Leung, 2008; McCready, 2004; Puar, 2007; Wilson, 1996, 2008). As a result, Brandon's narrative conflates his own experiences of marginalization as a white, gay, cisgender man with his own desire for more gay-specific services and supports in Toronto. It would seem that Brandon's image of gay organizations requires "gay" to be in the name of the services offered.

The centralization of gay, cisgender men within queer organizations also manifests through the job descriptions of helping professionals. As Steve, a 38-year-old gay, Latino, cisgender man who works as a sexual health coordinator at a large ASO explained, his job description requires him to "engage with gay men who are at risk of HIV and other STI infections and transmissions" (03/02/13, Transcript 20, p. 3, Toronto, ON). Within his role as a helping professional, Steve is required to home in on and centralize gay men and their sexual health risk within the programming and education initiatives he (and the organization) develops. Despite the particular constraints placed upon Steve, he spoke with me about how African women, Portuguese-speaking people, and refugees in Toronto are also impacted and affected by HIV/AIDS beyond the risk MSM presents. Connecting Steve's narrative to that of Indigenous peoples, his practice approach addresses, to some degree, how racism, mobility, and colonialism are social determinants of health. Even though Steve has demonstrated knowledge of the varying degrees to which health is impacted by racism, language, and country of origin, his narrative demonstrates the pervasiveness and power of Indigenous erasure in the context of queer organizations – what Morgensen (2011b) calls *settler homonationalism*. Later in our interview, Steve spoke to me about an awareness of Indigenous issues within his private practice as a therapist (but not in his role at the queer organization).

Additionally, Rahim, a 27-year-old gay/queer, South Asian, cisgender man who works as a prevention coordinator at a large sexual health organization discussed how, although his job description does explicitly outline gay and bisexual men as the primary population he is required to work with, he challenges this perception:

> I do a program ... it is about connecting guys who are taking high risks to community services and to provide a little bit of brief counseling ... usually creating a little bit of insight around what is going on for the person ... is it an informed choice ... what other things are impacting their decision making ... it could be substance use, relationship issues, or other structural things. (01/22/13, Transcript 10, p. 3, Toronto, ON)

Rahim's narrative illustrates how gay/queer helping professionals of colour can challenge the language around "risk" that is contained in their job description, indicating that one's sexual practices may not necessarily make them a target for risk. Rahim pointed out that risk is dependent upon the individual, interpersonal, and structural constraints service users live within. Rahim's narrative demonstrates how his job description, and thus the organization's mandate or focus, can be subverted as a way to decentre MSM within programming and the services he can offer. In doing so, Rahim tries to deploy a queer-of-colour critique to the program for guys who may not necessarily fall into the categories of, or want to classify themselves as, gay or bisexual.

Moving beyond HIV/AIDS discourses that centralize MSM, Emily, a 52-year-old, white, lesbian, cisgender woman who works as a director of programs at a large organization discussed how her organization tries "to serve the local community as well as the broader LGBTQ+ community" by doing and promoting "civic engagement, and involv[ing] the communities in the work that we do. We also provide programs and services to meet their needs" (12/23/12, Transcript 2, p. 3, Toronto, ON). The organization Emily works for has a plethora of programming and services that are directed towards serving divergent LGBTQ2S+ community members. Additionally, Nicole, a 46-year-old, queer, white, cisgender woman who works as a program coordinator at a youth organization discussed how the overall mission and mandate of her organization attempts to support divergent youth. As she stated: "[we] work with young queer, trans, and questioning youth up to the age [of] twenty-nine to help them find the tools and the resources to improve their lives, to advocate, to resist oppression, and to move forward in healthy ways" (03/13/13, Transcript 25, p. 3, Toronto, ON). Nicole speaks to the ways in which her organization works with a vast array of racially and ethnically diverse youth, empowering them to resist oppression and encouraging them to "move forward in healthy ways" (03/13/13, Transcript 25, p. 3, Toronto, ON). Nicole's narrative illustrates how queer organizations provide opportunities to push against the pervasive narrative that queer organizations largely encompass MSM, pointing to the various ways LGBTQ2S+ and questioning youth are supported and centred.

While attempts are made to foster relevant and meaningful programming and services within queer organizations, Josephine, a 33-year-old, queer, white, cisgender woman who works as a program coordinator at a large queer organization and Candy, a 27-year-old, South Asian, genderqueer person who works as a student intern at a large queer organization discussed the recent change their queer organization has made to their weekly drop-in. These two narratives illustrate how the name change of a program can have adverse, and sometimes even violent, consequences. As Josephine explained:

> In the fall we switched the focus [of the drop-in] a little bit so then it was more specifically geared to LGBT communities and allies. It was always

an open drop-in, but the intention with this switch was to hope to engage people more in creating safe space. We wanted people [coming to the drop-in] to commit to creating a safe space and to make it more inclusive for LGBTQ folks. I do not know if I am just noticing it more, or what is going on, but I feel like I am meeting so many more people [in the drop-in] who are LGBTQ and it is awesome. (01/09/13, Transcript 6, p. 3, Toronto, ON)

Josephine's story illuminated how her organization wanted to explicitly name their weekly drop-in as being for "LGBTQ and allies." Josephine spoke with me about how thrilled she was about the new change – it was an opportunity to make the space more accessible to and safer for LGBTQ2S+ service users, as well as their allies, who may not necessarily come or want to come to a more general weekly drop-in.

However, as Candy illustrated, the naming of the weekly drop-in as being for "LGBTQ and allies" has had violent repercussions for homeless service users – regardless of how they identify. As they went on to explain:

You know, changing the [weekly] drop-in to LGBTQ and allies ... they [the organization] do not understand homeless culture. It is rampedly [sic] homophobic. I get the intention that they want to create a safer space for LGBT people who are homeless or street involved. That totally makes sense if it was a shelter. Good idea, but it is not. [I am not sure if you know this], it was not published, but there was a gay bashing a month after we changed the program which has never happened before, ever ... ever. (01/15/13, Transcript 8, p. 5, Toronto, ON)

Candy's story outlined how queer organizations, through the specific naming of the weekly drop-in as being for "LGBTQ and allies," can have adverse and negative consequences. As Candy indicated, LGBTQ2S+ helping professionals, in deciding to make the drop-in even queerer at an already queer organization, did not consider the homeless service users who were already accessing and taking advantage of the drop-in. The overt naming and normalizing of a program as being for "LGBTQ and allies," as this particular event highlights, can have unfavourable and violent effects in terms of how inclusive language used within queer organizations can easily produce who belongs and who is deemed out of place. LGBTQ2S+ peoples and their perceived allies (whoever they may be) are made to belong, further oppressing poor people, people who are economically disenfranchised, and homeless people. What becomes remarkably clear within Candy's narrative is how the organization, in changing the name of the weekly drop-in to include "LGBTQ and allies," considered that its attendees' primary motivation to attend would be due to their gender and sexuality, rather than for shelter, access to food, community building, or the particular programming of that week.

Interestingly, Emily, a 52-year-old, white, cisgender lesbian who works as a director of programs at a large queer organization indicated that she sees Indigenous peoples accessing the drop-in among other services at the queer organization she works at. She went on to state:

> They [Aboriginal[2] people] come here. I think they go to other organizations too. I think that they go to all of the organizations that provide service that they might need. But I do not think that they are necessarily served well [here]. Or maybe there is something that we are missing, either in the kinds of services we offer or the ways that services are provided. Are we hiring Aboriginal staff? I know 2-Spirit people access some of our services, but I am unsure of the other services we offer. They are clearly accessing our programming that are serving very marginalized folks. (12/23/12, Transcript 2, p. 7, Toronto, ON)

Emily's narrative points to some of the structural limitations of queer organizations, in terms of organizations having the potential to be of disservice to, and possibly cause the erasure of, Indigenous service users. As a result of such limitations, the programming available to Indigenous peoples is operationalized around the perception that they require band-aid interventions for "marginalized folks" like drop-ins and food programs (see Kawash, 1998; Linklater, 2014; Rossiter, 2001). As Emily indicated, there are better and more specific services available to Indigenous service users in downtown Toronto that target "that population." Yet, Emily had noticed a stark gap between the services available to Indigenous service users generally and the specific queer services offered by the organization she works for.

The aforementioned participant narratives provide a glimpse into the compelling orientations of queer organizations, pointing to the ways gender and sexuality organize frontline and advocacy work. From the standpoint of the research participants themselves, the following stories shed light on the different ways queer organizations support and care for LGBTQ2S+ communities.

Providing Queer Services and Supports

Each of the research participants discussed the ways the queer organizations in Toronto provide support and services for LGBTQ2S+ communities. The following discussion evolved out of the research participants' lived experiences being LGBTQ+ and working in queer organizations, which effectively emerged and continue today to address the impact and effect of cisheterosexism within their daily lives.

Building Relationships and Counselling LGBTQ2S+ Peoples

The non-Indigenous LGBTQ+ helping professionals I spoke with discussed the formal and informal counselling services available to LGBTQ2S+ service users. Typically, these two types of counselling are accessed in various forms and modalities, given the variability in LGBTQ2S+ service users' experiences of trauma and violence (Hamilton & Mahalik, 2009; Ristock, 2001). Kate identified as a 25-year-old, bisexual/queer, white, cisgender woman and who works as a women's sexual-health coordinator at a sexual-health organization. Kate describes that she is involved with a queer organization that provides phone- and text-message-based crisis support services for LGBTQ2S+ and questioning youth. Kate's organization relies heavily on the labour of volunteers who are provided specific training for conducting over-the-phone crisis counselling. Kate notes that LGBTQ2S+ and questioning youth typically call into the queer organization to seek support and resources to "come out" to their parents or guardians, to discuss their gender expression or identity, and/or to question life (e.g., they may be contemplating suicide).

Also, Tara, a 29-year-old, white, genderqueer person who works as a program assistant at a mental-health organization, described the more formal LGBTQ2S+ counselling program offered at the organization they work for: "within that program, there are two smaller streams. One stream is for LGBTQ2S+ individuals, couples, and/or families. The second stream is for folks living with HIV or AIDS and people affected – so, people's partners, family members, friends" (05/06/13, Transcript 39, p. 3, Toronto, ON). Tara described the two types of counselling offered to LGBQ service users – one paid by the service user on a sliding scale, the other externally funded to support peoples living with or affected by HIV/AIDS. In our interview, Tara indicated that the majority of people accessing the HIV/AIDS services through their organization are white gay men and their partners. Tara also reported that the organization they work at is quite small and that, with limited resources, staff, and volunteers, the LGBTQ2S+ helping professionals often feel overburdened by the number of LGBTQ2S+ service users accessing counselling. Given the limited resources, staff, and volunteers, there is a waitlist for service users wanting to access counselling services.

Another interviewee, Jett, a 49-year-old, gay, white, cisgender man who works as an addictions counsellor at a large mental health organization, discussed the organization he works for as offering a few different types of counselling that mainly focus on addictions, stating: "we offer addictions programs for the LGBTQ2S+ community. We offer outpatient counselling, sometimes on a one-to-one basis. However, we are more of a group treatment program" (03/19/13, Transcript 28, p. 3, Toronto, ON). Substance use is known to be rampant in the LGBTQ2S+ communities in Toronto (and across North America) and is often used as an avenue to cope with multiple experiences of loss and trauma (Drable & Ellason, 2012; Hughes, 2005). As discussed in Chapter 4, Indigenous peoples may utilize alcohol as a strategy to cope with the ongoing effects of settler colonialism in their lives and communities. While substance use may be more prevalent within Indigenous communities (Vowel, 2016), Jett does not specifically engage LGBTQ2S+ Indigenous peoples in LGBTQ2S+ substance-use counselling work in his role. Instead, Jett works to support LGBTQ2S+ service users through a harm-reduction outpatient program or an abstinence-only inpatient program.

Lisa, a 46-year-old, mixed-race, cisgender lesbian who works as a newcomer service coordinator at a large organization, discussed how her organization operates quite differently in that she is required to work with LGBTQ+ newcomers who have decided to migrate or seek asylum in Canada. As she outlined: "I do one-on-one counselling with newcomers who are LGBTQ-identified and who have resided in Canada for less than five years" (13/01/15, Transcript 9, p. 5, Toronto, ON). Lisa described these "newcomers" – who are predominantly "convention refugees[3] or permanent residents who are not yet citizens" (13/01/15, Transcript 9, p. 5, Toronto, ON) – as populations that she helps and supports in traversing the Canadian immigration system and "Canadian culture" more generally. Lisa indicated to me that this particular service operates on a case-management basis to try to support refugees who have come to Canada as a result of experiencing violence in their homeland.

Lisa's role as a helping professional requires her to support "newcomers" as they navigate the white supremacist and colonial Canadian immigration system so that they can be read as legitimate, normative, LGBTQ2S+ subjects. Thus, counselling in this particular organization involves meeting with "newcomers" on a one-on-one basis to discuss how the organization can help support them in times of crisis, help them attain supporting documentation about permanent residency or full citizenship, and help integrate them into Canadian society. These research participants' narratives illustrate that counselling – crisis counselling, formal counselling, addictions counselling, and case management – is widely used to support and take care of LGBTQ2S+ service users. Next, I move to a discussion of some of the sexual and reproductive health services available within some queer organizations.

Sexual- and Reproductive-Health Services

Although counselling services may address aspects of sexual and repro-ductive healthcare, the following stories indicate why LGBTQ2S+-focused health services are necessary for LGBTQ2S+ service users, especially for cisgender and transgender women. As Brett, a 31-year-old, white, genderqueer person who works as a part-time relief worker at a sexual health organization, described, their role as a helping profes-sional requires them to provide

> services as fast, effectively, and as many as possible. I do HIV counseling and testing. This consists of pre-test counseling, the test itself and the post-counseling. I also do triaging: I get a person's sexual health history. I sug-gest the tests they should get done by the doctors, and then the doctor or clinician will come in, look at it, confirm everything or not, and then the person will do the actual tests. (04/30/13, Transcript 38, p. 4, Toronto, ON)

Brett's story illuminates how non-Indigenous LGBTQ2S+ helping pro-fessionals are put into authoritative positions whereby they are required to assess service users' sexual health and their potential risks. The goal of queer organizations, in Brett's case, is to provide predominantly GBTQ2S+ men with the opportunity to access free, nonjudgmental sexual-health services that are efficient, supportive, and informative. The information provided to LGBTQ2S+ male service is to help them make more informed choices about their own bodies and the bodies they interact with.

Additionally, April, a 30-year-old, white, genderqueer, person who works as a volunteer at a sexual-health organization, discussed a sexual- and reproductive-health service that predominantly serves LGBTQ2S+ women who are, in their estimation, free from cisheterosexism and pro-vides a safe, inclusive, and comfortable environment. As April stated: "I think those types of approaches are really unique, like that is not typically the experience when you get at your regular doctor or even a walk-in clinic … [laughs]" (06/05/13, Transcript 40, p. 3, Toronto, ON). April discussed the need for queer organizations to exist, insofar as LGBTQ2S+ women frequently experience sexual harassment and are explicitly asked intrusive heterosexist questions (e.g., do you have a boyfriend/husband; Fish, 2007; Peterson & Bricker-Jenkins, 1996). This particular queer service that April is involved with attempts to provide another avenue for LGBTQ2S+ women who may have had a bad experience with a doctor or other medical official or who want to avoid cis-heterosexist healthcare altogether. April's organization attempts to fill some gaps within the larger healthcare sector by attending to the health needs of, and thus caring for, LGBTQ2S+ women.

Sexual- and reproductive-health services provide support for LGBTQ2S+ service users that mainstream healthcare is ill-equipped to address. Queer organizations attempt to challenge the dominant healthcare paradigms by providing alternative and subversive spaces that value and care for LGBTQ2S+ service users. While queer organizations are trying to subvert mainstream healthcare practices by centring LGBTQ2S+ subjects, organizations are also travelling into schools and communities to educate LGBTQ2S+ people as well as the general cisheterosexual public on issues of health, sexuality, and gender identity.

Education

Many research participants spoke about how education, if used effectively, can challenge cisheteronormative perceptions of gender and sexuality. Kate, a 25-year-old bisexual/queer, white, cisgender woman who works as a women's sexual-health coordinator at a sexual-health organization discussed one of the roles at a queer organization that focused on LGBTQ2S+ women. Kate was tasked with connecting with LGBTQ2S+ women who are typically marginalized within queer organizations and discussing with them the types of education or training they would like to have access to, then attempting to meet their needs by developing workshops, events, and other educational programming.

Josh, a 53-year-old, queer, South Asian, cisgender man who works as a public educator at an Ontario-wide organization, spoke about a large responsibility he has as an educator at a large queer organization, stating: "I organize and create all the training. The education consists of building LGBT capacity for health care providers and social service workers to improve cultural competency in serving LGBTQ+ clients" (02/25/13, Transcript 17, p. 2, Toronto, ON). Josh's narrative suggests that there is a lack of awareness, particularly within a culturally competent approach within the helping professions, which can prevent LGBTQ2S+ service users from accessing mainstream healthcare and services. Josh travels and conducts workshops and training for primarily cisheterosexual healthcare worker audiences around building knowledge and cultural competency surrounding LGBTQ2S+ issues. Josh told me that within his workshops he does not shy away from discussions of race and explicitly chooses to include images of LGBTQ2S+ people of colour in his workshops.

Despite the active work done to *include* race under the auspice of cultural competency training, Josh also shared with me his scepticism of his colleagues and workshop attendees, being that he is the only queer person of colour in the organization, sharing that he often feels that it is his responsibility to discuss race, address racism, and educate his coworkers and workshop participants. Although Josh does not stray away from discussions of race or racism within his workshops with primarily cisheterosexual healthcare practitioners and other helping professionals, he did indicate that, when these types of LGBTQ2S+ capacity workshops are run, the topics of race or racism are typically removed by him in an attempt to home in on and question gender and sexuality.

Additionally, Dylan, a 25-year-old, queer, white, trans man who works as a volunteer at a youth organization, discussed with me his roles and responsibilities in volunteering. As he stated: "I am considered a facilitator. I go into schools, sometimes it is classes for social workers, but they are mostly middle schools and high schools to facilitate anti-oppression and anti-homophobia workshops" (04/15/13, Transcript 34, p. 2, Toronto, ON). Embedded within Dylan's narrative is the goal to address and educate young people on the oppressive realities faced by LGBTQ2S+ peoples, specifically the realities of homophobia and transphobia in schools. While these educational initiatives encourage LGBTQ2S+ helping professionals to learn about oppression and marginalization, which can act as a tool of empowerment, the resulting implications of "teaching about the Other" (Kumashiro, 2000) continue to place LGBTQ2S+ experiences and peoples generally as a phenomenon to be known.

These educational workshops continue to have tremendous impacts on attendees; they can easily drive queer organizations' agendas in centring a singular understanding of gender and sexuality, disconnected from other interlocutors. As Srivastava and Francis (2006) note: "in many contexts anti-racist and anti-homophobia workshops have been marked by techniques that allow white and/or straight participants to be passive or un-implicated while people of colour and/or queers are objects of interrogation and display" (p. 276). As a result, in relation to Josh's story, LGBTQ+ helping professionals of colour are invited to do away with an interlocking approach to, or queer-of-colour critique of, queer organizations by centralizing gender and sexuality alone. Unless non-Indigenous LGBTQ+ helping professionals themselves subvert the structural constraints placed upon them and their work, the resulting workshops can easily constrain what and who can be imagined as queer (see Cohen, 1997). The imaginations of queerness embedded within queer organizations can obscure the diverse and intersecting realities of LGBTQ2S+ people, which indeed do not necessarily fit neatly into a one- or two-hour workshop.

Conclusion

Queer organizations in downtown Toronto attempt to meet the needs of divergent LGBTQ2S+ service users who often experience marginalization and/or oppression due to their health status, gender identity or expression, and/or sexuality/sexual orientation. As demonstrated, the many queer organizations typically centre the health or identities of gay and bisexual cisgender men under the umbrella of reducing health risk, of programming initiatives, or of being within their job descriptions. Despite this, LGBTQ+ helping professionals of colour, such as Josh or Lisa, are subverting the structural confines of queer organizations to ensure that the needs of service users of colour are met – especially if they are migrants or seeking asylum. Importantly, the historical manifestation of queer organizations and their resulting contemporary realities construct a particular kind of LGBTQ2S+ identity – and that materializes itself in the wake of job descriptions, programming, and the bodies that enter into space. To echo Sara Ahmed (2012), the white walls of institutions often go unexamined. As a result, the work required to engage with "diversity" often is operationalized by inviting the Other in – often through a multicultural framework or through diversity work.

Chapter Two

"We Had the Rainbow": Queer Organizations and the Desire for White Settler Multiculturalism

Introduction

While queer organizations in Toronto offer an important intervention for cisheterosexism, specifically by providing counselling, healthcare services, and education, their investments in whiteness, nation-building, and multiculturalism often go unexamined. This chapter looks to the narratives of inclusion, diversity, and culture shared by non-Indigenous LGBTQ+ helping professions that shed light on how queer politics is imagined and enacted within queer organizations in Toronto. In 2012, gays and lesbians were included in Canada's definition of multiculturalism. For many LGBTQ2S+ peoples, similar to the removal of *homosexuality* from the DSM as noted in Chapter 1 or legalization of same-gender marriage, this is an important inclusionary step for the rights and freedoms of gays and lesbians; however, along with such acceptance and inclusion comes a particular imaginary of LGBTQ2S+ respectability and recognition. And, in including minoritized subjects like gays and lesbians into the status quo, many LGBTQ2S+ peoples can now invest in Canadian multiculturalism – which signals a larger investment in and promotion of Canada's commitment to diversity.

Vowel (2016) notes that the investment in the Canadian nation and the mantra of diversity and equality can obscure the historical and contemporary violence Indigenous peoples face. Thus, focusing on LGBTQ2S+ inclusion and acceptance under multiculturalism can obscure the white settler colonial conditions that were and continue to be founded upon the death, disappearance, and assimilation of Indigenous peoples, as well as the integration and torture of people of colour (Cannon & Sunseri, 2018; Razack, 2008; Razack et al., 2011; Sabzalian, 2019; Schick & McNinch, 2009; Thobani, 2007). As such, the imagined gays and lesbians included within this new envisioning of Canadian multiculturalism are considered nationals who benefit from and contribute to the Canadian economy and political life – and to Canada's image of itself.

The inclusion of gays and lesbians in official multiculturalism acts to shift popular perceptions around desiring and needing diversity, especially within queer organizations, rather than challenging the ways diversity (often coded as multiculturalism or vice versa) is used to sustain racial difference and white settler colonial oppression. The use of diversity within the national order of things can obscure the ways that queer organizations in Toronto are deeply embedded in and sustain whiteness. To address this oversight, this chapter asks: in what ways is the discourse of diversity used and imagined by non-Indigenous LGBTQ+ helping professionals working within queer organizations? Moreover, what consequences does the discourse of diversity hold for Indigenous peoples and people of colour? There is a paradox surrounding multicultural diversity: queer organizations utilize the language of diversity as a way to interpolate racial and cultural difference into queerness itself, and simultaneously these queer organizations innocently frame their internal organizing efforts within the lexicon of whiteness.

To examine how the discourse of diversity is used and (re)appropriated by non-Indigenous LGBTQ+ helping professionals, I begin by briefly outlining how diversity is shaped by official multicultural discourse in Canada. Further, I discuss the ways that queer politics and communities rely on inclusion, recognition, and diversity. Next, I situate the narratives of non-Indigenous LGBTQ+ helping-professional research participants within a larger theoretical discussion of the discourse of diversity. Finally, the implications of *desiring diversity* within queer communities and queer organizations in Toronto are addressed. Overall, this chapter addresses the ways multiculturalism in Canada is engaged by helping professionals and how it plays out within queer organizations through the use of diversity as a tactic to create further exclusion.

Multiculturalism, Inclusion, and the Discourse of (Queer) Diversity

Multiculturalism emerged in Canada in 1971, first as a policy under Prime Minister Pierre Elliot Trudeau and second, in 1988, as law within the official Multicultural Act under Prime Minister Brian Mulroney to address linguistic, cultural, and land-based disputes within the nation (Day, 2000; Mackey, 2002; St. Denis, 2011). Multiculturalism was first implemented as an imagined and very real creation of a cultural mosaic[1] – a strategic move away from the United States' melting pot[2] (Dion, 2009; Mackey, 2002; Simpson et al., 2011). This move created a falsified image of Canada (and its people) that is deeply rooted in notions of white innocence, whereby Canada has *only* taken part in peaceful engagements with Indigenous peoples and has never engaged in racism within its immigration practices. While research (see Cannon & Sunseri, 2018; Razack, 2002; Thobani, 2007) has documented the realities of racism and settler colonialism in Canada's history and present, the construction of a good and innocent Canadian citizen remains deeply entrenched in the imagery of Canada itself. Multiculturalism, in other words, was meant to enter into the fabric of everyday life to "design a unified nation" (Chazan et al. 2011, p. 3). As Rinaldo Walcott (2011) argued, multiculturalism has indeed become the "fundamental characteristic of Canadian heritage and identity" (p. 136).

Multiculturalism allows Canadian citizen-subjects to erase historical and contemporary white-supremacist and settler colonial processes and practices. As Sunera Thobani (2007) so aptly put it, "multiculturalism allowed Canadians to resolve the crisis of whiteness through its [Canada's] reorganization as tolerant, pluralist and racially innocent, uncontaminated by its previous racist history" (p. 154). The ideological and discursive use of multiculturalism produces a Canada that is inclusive, diverse, and tolerant and that "celebrat[es] ... differences" (Dion, 2009, p. 74). This particular mantra of celebration has become the central pillar for constructing a Canadian national identity. Within this celebration of differences lies an essential homogenization of the population, creating a core Canadian culture whereby Indigenous peoples and people of colour have been made to become Others within the nation. Multiculturalism has been put in place to manage the country's internal differences by maintaining its core culture – a white settler nation established by the "founding nations" (the British and French) (Day, 2000; Mackey, 2002; Thobani, 2007; Walcott, 2011). In sustaining narratives and imaginations of early conquest, this core culture places the power and control into the hands of whites, while Others – those who are BIPOC – are considered secondary, included within the nation so long as they assimilate and become "Canadian" (Greensmith & Sheppard, 2018). Thus, multiculturalism is used to bring multilinguistic, multiracial, and multicultural differences together under the rubric of diversity, and anyone who exists outside of this narrative is required to assimilate and is simultaneously constructed as an outsider due to their culture (Bannerji, 2000; Razack, 2008).

Many Indigenous scholars have argued that the particular focus on multiculture is the mechanism that erases Indigenous peoples' unique articulations of nationhood and sovereignty by requiring an investment in white settler colonial institutions (e.g., The Indian Act) (Cannon & Sunseri, 2018; Coulthard, 2007; Lawrence & Dua, 2005; Sabzalian, 2019; St. Denis, 2011). Leilani Sabzallian (2019) argues that the discourse of multiculturalism "ignores the political (or multinational) diversity of Indigenous peoples" (p. 312) and conflates "race and Indigeneity" (p. 314). Moreover, as Thobani (2007) notes, "state-sponsored multiculturalism compels [Indigenous peoples] to negotiate and comprehend their identities on very narrow grounds, discouraging and possibly foreclosing the possibility of alliances that might allow a systemic challenge to white dominance, patriarchy, and global corporate capitalism" (p. 175). Multiculturalism erases Indigenous peoples' experiences of white settler colonialism to trace them as belonging to a "special interest group" that is produced as one cultural group among many (Cannon & Sunseri, 2018; Lawrence & Dua, 2005; Porter, 1999; St. Denis, 2011; Thobani, 2007). The sole focus on culture erases the divergent struggles among BIPOC while perpetuating the common understanding of communities as distinctly and culturally separate.

The power of multiculturalism sustains cultural differences in Canada. Eva Mackey (2002) provided a rich analysis of Canadian "core identity" as being comprised of "Canadian-Canadians," a term used by white people interviewed to indicate their ordinariness – an "unmarked, non-ethnic, and usually white ... identity" (p. 20). As a result of such conceptualizations, the (presumed) whiteness of nationals becomes normalized, effectively producing BIPOC as "Others" (Ahmed, 2000). This has grave consequences for how Canadian identity is regulated and policed. The assimilation required of Indigenous peoples and people of colour produces Canada and its imaginings of citizenship as only white (Greensmith & Sheppard, 2018). The presence of BIPOC within this nation that is "celebrating of difference" continues to be viewed as compromising the whiteness of the Canadian nation state (Thobani, 2007).

In other words, "multiculturalism is itself a politic of settlement" (Chazan et al. 2011, p. 1). While evocations of diversity and difference invite Canadian citizen-subjects to desire the allure of multiculturalism, the process of white settlement through which Canada was founded remains immune from scrutiny. Indeed, the use of diversity – requiring, needing, and wanting diversity – obscures the realities of the structural whiteness embedded within institutions and organizations (Ahmed, 2012). Instead of working towards challenging structures of domination that continue to deride and repudiate the well-being of BIPOC, diversity is used to bring attention to difference – attention that can emerge as an empty gesture of inclusion or a problematic politics of recognition, as will be discussed later. It is thus through the discourse of diversity – and the desire for it – that the Canadian nation state holds whiteness at its centre by portraying cultural/racial groups as Others who are at once celebrated and marginalized due to their differences (Greensmith & Sheppard, 2018). Under multiculturalism, difference and diversity are produced as desirable for the nation but also for its citizens, which many helping professionals adopt as they attempt to be "culturally competent."

Cultural competency can be defined as "a set of congruent behaviours, attitudes, and policies that come together in a system, agency, or among professionals and enable that system, agency or those professionals to work effectively in cross-cultural situations" (Cross et al., 1989, p. iv). Cultural competency encourages helping professionals to "develop sensitivity towards, appreciation for, understanding of and knowledge about" service users they are working with and helping (Schick & McNinch, 2009, p. xiii). However, cultural-competency training and workshops also have the tendency to enact what Kevin Kumashiro (2000) calls "education about the Other," which assumes the modernist goal of having full knowledge of and seeking the truth about the Other. Carol Schick and James McNinch (2009) caution against the use of cultural competency as it has the potential to delegitimize and downplay the realities of racism and colonialism experienced by BIPOC.

As Carmela Murdocca (2009) explains: "Aboriginal peoples are locked into the inevitability of inclusion through a paradigm of culture, [which] operate[s] to promote a sense of national benevolence" (p. 27). Locking BIPOC into positions to be known, on the part of helping professionals, can easily sustain white settler colonial projects and the cultural erosion of Indigenous peoples (Murdocca, 2009). All helping professionals can participate in, take on, and challenge their approach to know difference and diversity under cultural competency logics embedded within helping professions. As Gordon Pon (2009) has theorized, cultural competency essentializes the experiences of racialized and colonized peoples. Pon notes that cultural competency is a new form of racism coded as culture and used to mask the realities of white supremacy and colonialism embedded within social work and other helping professions. Cultural competency can create a "one size fits all," cookie-cutter approach to service delivery that creates the illusion that everyone will be treated the same (Yee & Dumbrill, 2003). As Verna St. Denis (2007) theorized, cultural competency relies on the deficit construction of Indigenous peoples and encourages "the [popular] belief that the cultural difference of the Aboriginal 'Other' is the problem" (p. 1086).

The popular use of cultural competency within the helping professions erases how organizations themselves are already embedded in
reproducing white-supremacist and settler colonial understandings of
BIPOC. As Donna Jeffery (2009) noted:

> It is easier to include aboriginal peoples, immigrants, and people of colour
> into social work stories, practices and structures of finding new ways to
> help the disadvantaged and marginalized, than it is to reconfigure the
> story of social work itself as a *story of white supremacy, because that is an
> unappealing story of complicity*. (p. 445; emphasis added)

Jeffery argued that utilizing cultural competency requires helping professionals to understand the culture of those whom they help as static.
Pon (2009) has urged helping professionals to let go of their desire for
a cultural-competency approach. The desire on the part of helping professionals to know diversity under multiculturalism is deeply embedded within a politics of recognition and knowing difference through
racial descriptors of nonwhiteness.

Nancy Fraser's (2000) theorization of recognition becomes useful
in thinking through the ways diversity is utilized within the helping
professions generally and queer organizations in Toronto. In particular,
for Fraser, recognition naturalizes the production of difference where
being recognized is only validated through the act of naming. A politics
of naming allows for the subject to be differentiated while simultaneously constituted as different through that very process (Ahmed, 2000).
So, bringing this all back to the concept of diversity, this comes to mean
many things but typically resides within the recognition of culture,
whereby BIPOC come to exist on the colonizers' terms alone. In other
words, diversity further normalizes racial and settler colonial hierar-
chies, which emphasizes the capacity of white settlers to recognize and
know culture (Coulthard, 2007; Povinelli, 2002).

Jett, a 49-year-old, gay, white, cisgender man who works as an addictions counsellor at a large mental-health organization, when respond-
ing to one of my questions, discussed the diversity among service users
accessing services at the organization he works at:

Q: Who are the service users at your agency?
A: We see all kinds of people. The people we never have problems getting
   in as clients are gay men. Even if we did not advertise or do outreach,
   we still would have a ton of gay men coming in. So a lot of the groups
   that we have available at [the organization] are geared to gay guys. That
   being said we see lots of women. Within both the men's and women's

community, we see some diversity. We have quite a lot of Asian clients. We see a fair number of Black clients. We see fewer Aboriginal clients. (03/19/13, Transcript 28, p. 5, Toronto, ON)

Jett's narrative points to how helping professionals, and indeed queer organizations, are representing and including the concept of diversity. Jett was able to utilize racial descriptors of nonwhiteness to describe the service users accessing addiction services at his organization. In his estimation, there were some "Asian" and "Black" service users but fewer "Aboriginal" service users accessing addiction services. In using these particular racial markers of nonwhiteness without provocation, Jett illustrated how the category "gay" he evoked remained white unless specifically delineated to include people of colour and Indigenous peoples – a common trope helping professionals of colour shared with me and were actively working against in their work.

As Glen Coulthard (2007) noted, the politics of recognition is used to downplay Indigenous peoples as subjects who self-determine, further naturalizing ongoing genocide and conquest of Indigenous peoples and nations in Canada. And, while the politics of recognition is entrenched within the discourse of diversity contained in helping professionals' imaginings of difference, it also plays out and operates differently within Toronto's queer spaces, places, and organizations. Thus, returning to the object of inquiry – queer organizations – they participate in and prop up the politics of recognition as they come to know the cultural difference as a set of skills or competencies. The desire to be recognized, and name, on the part of helping professionals, is an important aspect of multiculturalism, within which (certain) inclusive queer politics reside.

As David Eng (2010) contended, within mainstream queer politics, racial differences are routinely denied – meaning that race itself becomes erased in the processes and practices that foster individual freedom and merit within the nation state. This has consequences for people's identity as BIPOC. Queer liberalism – the "contemporary confluence of the political and economic spheres that forms the basis for liberal inclusion of particular gay and lesbian U.S. [and Canadian] citizen-subjects petitioning for rights and recognition before the law" (Eng, 2010, p. 3) – has transformed queer organizations, movements, and politics in Toronto, causing them to rely heavily on state forms of recognition. These legal forms of queer recognition, deeply tied to the politics of recognition (Ahmed, 2000; Coulthard, 2007; Fraser, 2000; Povinelli, 2002), are amplified within queer organizations in that they perpetuate and normalize the neoliberal understanding that each citizen-subject has the same rights, freedoms, and opportunities and should invest in and maintain a commitment to the nation state (Eng, 2010; Greensmith, 2015; Reddy, 2011).

Tara, a 29-year-old, white, genderqueer person who works as a program assistant at a mental-health organization, discussed with me how the counsellors within their organization work against such narratives. As they shared:

> Every time a state passes a marriage bill that is the only thing that my manager will talk about. I think the counselors have been asked by the board of directors why it is still useful to have a queer counseling service when gay rights have gone so far so they are fighting, I think, against that narrative. (05/06/13, Transcript 39, p. 6, Toronto, ON)

With the increasing enfoldment of equality discourses and respectable queerness into the Canadian nation state and across the United States, Tara's coworkers are routinely required to justify why queer counselling remains necessary for LGBTQ2S+ service users. Importantly, Tara's story illuminates a tension within queer organizations: the *queerness* within queer organizations requires a focus on gay-rights discourses, such as passing of a marriage bill. Chandan Reddy (2011) notes that "to seek full inclusion within the modern state ... will do little to change the conditions by which legitimate violence continues to be naturalized" (p. 39). Consequently, the discursive and material realities of white settler multiculturalism are utilized to erase the powerful structural inequalities used to conflate queerness with whiteness, continuing the phenomenon that "queer is a white thing" (Muñoz, 1999, p. 9).

Contemporary queer organizations and communities in Toronto are not immune to such processes even as they invest in and desire diversity. Diversity here is used as a way of upholding whiteness: BIPOC are always having to prove that they are *queer enough*. The idea of one's queerness needing to be justified fits within Puar's (2007) theorization of the politics of recognition whereby queer politics is based upon the concept of sustaining difference. To be queer must

> entail that certain ... homosexual, gay, and queer bodies may be temporary recipients of the 'measures of benevolence' that are afforded by liberal discourses of multicultural tolerance and diversity. This benevolence towards sexual others is contingent upon ever-narrowing parameters of white racial privilege, consumption, capabilities, gender and kinship normativity, and bodily integrity. (Puar, 2007, p. xii)

The nature of multiculturalism's prerequisite for diversity within such evocations of Canadian queer politics has moved ideological and discursive frameworks towards inclusion – founded upon a "politics of colorblindness" (Eng, 2010, p. x). Thus, to be included under the queer rainbow requires folks marked with a difference to rid themselves of their differences or assimilate so that they become legible as queer. This tactic of assimilation mimics the larger multicultural ideologies in Canada that ask BIPOC to minimize the white racism and settler colonialism they encounter and embed themselves within a unified or homogeneous queer community. A look at specific examples within the Canadian queer imaginary helps bring out this point.

Pride Toronto, a large not-for-profit organization, organizes a yearly week-long celebration and weekend-long parade (which did not occur in 2020 due to the global pandemic caused by the virus COVID-19) with related events that coincide with themes intended to unify often-divergent LGBTQ2S+ peoples, communities, and organizations. Many of the research participants I spoke to noted that their organization would set out information booths. Despite this intention to create and foster inclusion and acceptance, many LGBTQ2S+ BIPOC can often find attending Pride Toronto to be incredibly isolating and unsafe (Greensmith & Giwa, 2013). Giwa and I (2012) have noted that Pride Toronto festivals and events attempt to showcase LGBTQ2S+ communities in the best possible light, whereby any racism experienced by queer/gay men of colour is often downplayed. Moreover, as Giwa and I (2013) have articulated, Pride Toronto's festivals and events not only reproduce racism but also settler colonialism through the erasure of 2-Spirited presence and the eroticization of Indigeneity. 2-Spirit peoples' everyday life is impacted by settler homonationalism, since they continue to "experience a degree of racism that is reminiscent of heteropatriarchal society" (Wolfe, 2013, p. 16). The persistence of settler colonialism within Pride Toronto is exemplified in Raven's (a research participant) story of an underwear contest, whereby the *sexy* presence of Indigeneity was relocated to a headdress, thereby perpetuating stereotypical representations that work to enable Indigenous peoples' dispossession (Greensmith & Giwa, 2013).

In the summer of 2016, #BlackLivesMatter (BLM)-TO stopped the Sunday parade to hold a teach-in to address the overt and covert ways anti-Black racism is entrenched within Pride Toronto (e.g., the defunding of Blockorama and the heightened presence of Toronto police at the parade) and in Toronto's LGBTQ2S+ communities. One of many demands "was [a] ban on police forces marching in uniform or full regalia and carrying guns at the parade" (Walcott, 2017). Moreover, as Walcott (2017) notes:

> The coordination between BLM-TO and the Indigenous community signalled a different relationship to contemporary politics. It signalled that Black and Indigenous activists and thinkers are seeking ways to work together that bridge white liberal divides that seek to separate us. And what more powerful way to demonstrate that bridge than to come together around policing at Pride [Toronto]? The power of the continuous Indigenous drumming kept us centered in the righteousness of demands within our sit-down protest.

Despite these calls to action and relationships built between Black and Indigenous peoples, in 2019 Pride Toronto issued a formal "LAND ACKNOWLEDGEMENT:"

> What is that? Let us journey together ...
>   Take a moment to connect with the land that you are currently standing on.
>   Now introduce yourself spiritually: build a relationship with Mother Earth that provides for all our relations.
>   No matter what part of Mother Earth our family originates from, we all have a relationship and responsibility to the land.
>   Let's build a healthy relationship together.
>   CHI MIIGWECH. (CBC NEWS, 2019)

While Pride Toronto states that an Indigenous person wrote the land acknowledgment, much criticism can be directed at the erasure of the specific nations (e.g., Anishinaabe, Mississaugas, and Haudenosaunee) and the concern that local Indigenous peoples and communities were not notified regarding the land acknowledgment or the ways the land acknowledgment can fit within larger discourses of inclusion or diversity that can erase any real or sustained attempt to decolonize. As Sabzalian (2019) argues, Indigenous self-determination and sovereignty are not synonymous with multicultural inclusion or rights frameworks. It is also concerning that, with many supports available to non-Indigenous peoples to appropriately and ethically acknowledge the territories in which they reside, Pride Toronto still felt the need to have an Indigenous person create the land acknowledgment. These examples from Pride Toronto festivals and event programming provide a glimpse into the ways Toronto LGBTQ2S+ communities, organizations, and politics are messy and temporally specific and expose the embedded racial and settler colonial power relations embedded therein.

Articulations and evocations of LGBTQ2S+ politics and identities are also made possible through investments in the Canadian nation state that paint queer people and people of colour as "risky" subjects. For example, as outlined on the Canadian Blood Services (CBS) (2017a; 2017b) website, MSM and trans people are historically and contemporarily produced as at risk for acquiring HIV/AIDS, due to the presumption that they are having unprotected sex. As a result, these groups are unable to donate blood until they have abstained from oral or anal sex for a minimum of 12 months (CBS, 2017a, 2017b). Also, people coming from HIV-endemic countries (such as Togo or Cameroon) are forced to defer their donation of blood due to their (presumed) greater risk of acquiring different and more rare strains of HIV (CBS, 2017c). Thus, MSMs, trans people, and people from HIV-endemic countries are perceived to be, and treated as, risky subjects. Omisoore Dryden (2010) has discussed the larger implications of particular groups being marked as respectable blood-donation subjects who should thus be donating their blood in Canada.

Dryden contended "[CBS] positions the blood donor as heroic, generous, selfless, thoughtful and moral" (p. 78) – traits that resemble the larger narratives of Canadian citizen-subjects and their benevolent attachments to white settler goodness. Here, the subject who should be donating blood is one who has not compromised their health status, producing a group of "risky" subjects – those who are LGBTQ2S+ and/ or Black – who might compromise both the blood of the nation and the respectable politics of blood donation. Dryden illustrates that the association of risk with the LGBTQ2S+ and/or Black body presumes that they have somehow come into contact with HIV (e.g., through having multiple sex partners or being from an HIV-endemic country). This categorization produces the white and/or straight subject as free from risk – even though we know that these categories of identity are socially constructed, permeable, and ever-shifting (see Ward, 2015). In this production of LGBTQ2S+ and/or Black subjects as risky, the potential links between queerness and Blackness remain erased. In doing so, those "just gay" subjects are "produced through the occlusion of whiteness as a racial category" (Dryden, 2010, p. 5). It is through this mechanism that the "just gay" subject becomes the subject worthy of intervention, while the (LGBTQ+)-Black subject continues to be constructed as always risky due to their Blackness and presumed geographical positioning as an outsider.

As Koinnapat, a 35-year-old gay/queer, East Asian, cisgender man who works as a volunteer at a sexual health organization, discussed, queer organizations remain white, despite steps towards diversity and inclusion. In our conversation about racism, Koinnapat noted: "I think [some organizations] need to do a lot more to address the specific cultural needs of different groups and have some honest conversations about the racism in the [LGBTQ+] community" (02/02/13, Transcript 11, p. 3, Toronto, ON). Koinnapat talked about the complete whitewashing of queer organizations in Toronto, as seen in their inability to meet the needs of service users of colour, let alone Back or Indigenous service users. Moreover, Koinnapat discussed how actions used to address white racism seem to be absent within queer organizations: "I think the more mainstream organizations should be reaching out but they are not" (02/02/13, Transcript 11, p. 10, Toronto, ON). From Koinnapat's standpoint, mainstream queer organizations are not addressing race or racism in a real or meaningful way, let alone Indigenous identity and decolonization, because there are ethno-specific agencies considered specialized enough to speak to and work towards eliminating racism.

The Desire for Multicultural Diversity and Difference

A deeper examination of how diversity and difference are evoked by non-Indigenous LGBTQ+ helping professionals within Toronto's queer service sector follows. I pay attention to discourses of diversity used within the queer organizations to represent and understand the difference by illustrating how many of the non-Indigenous LGBTQ+ research participants centre whiteness in their attempts to appear and become inclusive. While non-Indigenous LGBTQ+ helping professionals articulate their investments in diversity, it is important to situate their narratives within the larger culture (organization and nation state) that props up multiculturalism as how difference is to be understood and engaged.

Filipe, a 46-year-old, gay/queer, Portuguese, cisgender man who works as a sexual health coordinator at a large ASO, discussed how program advertising campaigns, such as one targeting youth, can exclude Indigenous peoples by using the word "diversity." As he stated:

When you look at that poster on your door, it says something about diverse communities. That is code and usually it means multi-ethnicity. A lot of white people feel that [diversity] does not mean them. A lot of ethno-specific people think that means everyone. So what does diversity mean to First Nations people? Because First Nations people do not necessarily see themselves as being ethno-specific, they are First Nations. So to be truly accessible to First Nations people we should be putting First Nations on that poster. 'Diverse' does not cover it and I am very aware of that. (03/15/13, Transcript 27, p. 7, Toronto, ON)

Filipe's story connects to Sara Ahmed's (2012) theorization of the use of "diversity" within higher education as a way to direct attention towards racial inclusivity and away from the structural apparatuses that continue to reify white supremacy. *Diversity*, in the case of Filipe's queer organization's program poster, has multiple meanings depending on one's social location and overall knowledge of diversity. As the narratives of many non-Indigenous research participants suggest, this particular queer organization continues to be white-normed by the service users who access the organization and the helping professionals who work there – despite the organization's claim to serve diverse populations within Toronto's "queer community."

Discussing a different queer organization in Toronto, Lisa, a 46-year-old, mixed-race, cisgender woman and lesbian who works as a newcomer service coordinator, suggested: "over the years [the organization] gained a reputation as a male gay white space. We have developed into a more inclusive, diverse space for every single population to be able to find a program or a space to feel recognized, valued, positive and to be engaged" (01/15/13, Transcript 9, p. 6, Toronto, ON). As Lisa points out, queer organizations, such as the one she works at, use "diversity" as a way to showcase their inclusivity practices and seeming ability to include all populations within the services and programming offered. As Filipe suggested, the inclusion of diversity alone can do a disservice to Indigenous peoples recognizing themselves within queer organizations. The use of diversity within a Canadian queer imaginary ensures that Indigenous peoples are represented as another cultural group among many (Cannon & Sunseri, 2018; Lawrence & Dua, 2005; St. Denis, 2011). Filipe and Lisa's discussion of diversity within their queer organizations illustrates that the imaginary of diversity is not enough of an inclusionary measure to include difference and that, if queer organizations want to truly support Indigenous peoples' self-determination and sovereignty, they must meaningfully decolonize their programming and advertisements.

While Lisa acknowledges that her organization was once white-normed and focused on gay men, she notes that the organization has changed significantly to include many populations, including her "newcomer" program. Ryan, a 34-year-old, gay, white, cisgender man with Indigenous ancestry[3] who works as a sexual health counsellor at a sexual health organization, discussed the disproportionate number of "privileged" service users coming into his organization to access HIV and STI testing versus more marginalized groups. As he stated: "I think the people that we see are a split of 60/40 – [MSM] and women who have sex with women. That number is so *crazily* disproportionate if you look at [the] overall representation [of people newly diagnosed with HIV]" (13/03/09, Transcript 23, p. 6, Toronto, ON). As a helping professional involved with Indigenous sexual-health initiatives in the City of Toronto, Ryan remained cognizant of the degree to which Indigenous peoples in Toronto are being newly diagnosed with HIV. However, even with his knowledge of HIV/AIDS in urban Indigenous communities, Ryan, in his role as a helping professional, had little individual control over who actually sees themselves part of, and ultimately enters, the organization.

Brandon, a 53-year-old, gay, white, cisgender man who works as a community-based researcher at a large ASO, discussed the service users who attend the workshops he facilitates: "people who are HIV positive gay men. I would say most of those programs would have maybe Caucasian guys but it is diverse. Within the other programs that I do it is a wide diversity – all kinds of ethnicities" (03/09/13, Transcript 22, p. 7, Toronto, ON). Brandon spoke of both white male participants and male participants of colour, indicating that he was cognizant of racialized people accessing programming. Brandon's narrative depicts how the language of diversity as code for ethnicity or race can be incomplete when naming who typically access services or workshops.

Similarly, Jacob, a 20-year-old, gay/queer, Portuguese, cisgender man who works as a support worker at a large ASO, discussed the service users at the organization he worked at:

[We see] trans guys, HIV positive and HIV negative guys. We also see guys from any and all ethnic backgrounds. Although there is this assumption that Aboriginal people will fall under that last category, it is not explicitly stated. I think that explains a lack of presence of Aboriginal participants in the program. (03/13/13, Transcript 24, p. 4, Toronto, ON)

Jacob's narrative extends the version of "gay" mobilized by the queer organization he works within to expand the use of diversity to include gender and ethnicity variance. Within Jacob's narrative, like Filipe, he recognized that Indigenous peoples might not necessarily see themselves in the category of "ethnicity." Interestingly, his evocation of "any and all ethnic backgrounds" connects to discussions of cultural competency and other diversity or inclusion practices and pedagogies, whereby all helping professionals can easily erase experiences with racism and colonialism in an attempt to gloss over differences that exist among the umbrella of diversity. Jacob's narrative illustrates how the use of ethnicity can erase Indigenous peoples since Indigenous peoples do not necessarily see themselves as represented within the category of "ethnicity" used to include racial and cultural differences within queer organizations.

Joseph, a 47-year-old, queer, white, genderqueer person who works as a community-based researcher at a large ASO, echoed Steve's narrative, particularly in their discussion of how Indigenous/2-Spirit peoples can assimilate into "gay" programming. As they stated:

> Aboriginal folks can also be poz [HIV positive] and queer, [so] they [can] fit into my poz work, which is not limited to gay men. Although, my gay male [workshop] is limited to gay men. Some Aboriginal folks may not identify as gay men, they may identify as 2-Spirit and those may be two distinct things for them. That is their identity and I am okay with that. So [in] our gay men's group they are most welcome but if they are not feeling that they are gay male identified then maybe the program is not best for them ... and [then we] think about connecting them to an Aboriginal ASO or an Aboriginal organization to validate the Aboriginal identity experience. (02/13/13, Transcript 15, p. 6, Toronto, ON)

Joseph discussed with me how Indigenous peoples fit into the work that they do. Joseph's narrative defends the existence of gay male programming where 2-Spirit people might not necessarily fit by understanding them as finding little refuge in gay male programming; as a result, it is thought that they can simply access other ("Aboriginal") programming (Wilson, 1996). The inclusion of "2-Spirited" identity in "gay male" programming, in Joseph's experience, seems to be conditional upon static identity categories like "gay" that can easily constrain who can ever feel like they belong within programming.

Interviews with participants also uncovered gestures of recognition made by organizations that bring with them not only a sense of pointlessness but also further erasure of 2-Spiritedness. My interaction with Robert, a 32-year-old, white, queer, trans man who works as a health coordinator at a healthcare organization, demonstrated how the imagery of 2-Spiritedness, using the 2 Spirited People of the First Nations (2-Spirits) [45] flag, can be included in the form of a poster to signal the organization's claims to diversity and yet, when examined more closely, can remain disconnected from the bodies on the poster:

> Q: I see that there is a [2-Spirits] flag on that poster.
> A: Interesting.
>
> Q: [Names poster title].
> A: Yes – I have actually never noticed that before and it is not like it is above a picture of people who identify as 2-Spirit. I know most of these people personally and none of them identify as 2-Spirit. So what the hell is it doing there? (02/07/13, Transcript 13, p. 28, Toronto, ON)

As Robert pointed out, the recognition of 2-Spirits seems additive, as none of the people in the poster self-identify as Indigenous or 2-Spirit, nor do they have Indigenous ancestry. Although Robert's queer organization attempted to include Indigenous peoples in the form of a 2-Spirits flag; its inclusion showcases how celebrations of diversity in the form of recognizable Indigenous difference on a poster can disconnect queer organizations and non-Indigenous LGBTQ+ helping professionals from engaging in critiques of white settler colonialism within their institutional walls – mimicking the multicultural apparatus of the nation state. The imagery of a 2-Spirits flag becomes an empty gesture used to signal the "celebration of diversity" without meaningful engagement with decolonial practices. Here diversity is used to obscure the queer organizations' investments in white queerness by bringing attention to diversity without addressing the larger structural realities in which queer organizations are embedded.

A focus on diversity itself within these organizations was exemplified by Eric, a 39-year-old, gay, white, cisgender man who works as a volunteer at a healthcare organization, who discussed with me the demographics of presenters at workshops he had organized. As he went on to explain: "[we] had the rainbow. The Asian, the Black person, the Latino. However, [we] did not have an Aboriginal person" (03/29/13, Transcript 33, p. 5, Toronto, ON). Although "diversity" was achieved in the form of "the rainbow," as Eric noted, Indigenous peoples and perspectives were not present or considered relevant. In connection with larger projects of Canadian multiculturalism, to be truly diverse the workshop would need to have perspectives from as many racial and cultural groups as possible. Eric's discussion of "the rainbow" as representative of diversity brings to the forefront how racial or ethnic diversity can easily end at a checklist, whereby diversity is achieved when (some) bodies of people of colour are included. Moreover, the discourse of diversity in Eric's iteration of the rainbow can easily inhibit non-Indigenous LGBTQ+ helping professionals from understanding how the institution in which they work normalizes white settler colonialism functionality.

Directing one's gaze towards diversity itself, as Ahmed (2012) argued, diverts attention from the structural realities that facilitate the normalization of white supremacy. These stories that the research participants shared with me illustrate how the desire for diversity within queer organizations can obscure the ways white supremacy and settler colonial oppression operate within and between queer organizations. Calling attention to needing, wanting, and desiring of diversity within Toronto's queer organizations opens up spaces to challenge these taken-for-granted forms of LGBTQ2S+ recognition and inclusion that are appropriated by helping professionals and institutions they work within.

Conclusion: Inclusivity and the Reproduction of Queer Settler Whiteness

The stories of diversity discussed in this chapter showcase how non-Indigenous LGBTQ+ helping professionals working within queer organizations are propelled into sustaining projects of Canadian nation-building, which their work indeed supports. After all, the goal of queer organizations, as documented in Chapter 1, is to support, help, and care for as many divergent LGBTQ2S+ service users and community members as possible. Yet, in making Indigenous peoples an exception within the concept of diversity, queer organizations can easily normalize white settler queerness within the walls of their institutions.

The narratives of the research participants provide an opportunity to consider how diversity is used as a mechanism to sustain difference – naming white LGBTQ+ people specifically as within the discourse of diversity. Here, the assumption is that non-Indigenous LGBTQ+ people do not *require* diversity – they are imagined as part of the very fabric of Canadian identity, as Fitzgerald and Rayter (2012) argue. Thus, only people of BIPOC, where diversity is pinned onto their bodies, require the recognition of white (queer) settlers to know diversity. BIPOC are then perceived as the Other: they are invited to participate in and utilize the supports and services of queer organizations, but if they require additional programming or "specialized services" outside of the queer lexicon, they are encouraged to access those through separate ethno-specific or "cultural" organizations. Sustaining this difference through diversity maintains the status quo: the whiteness of queerness is deeply embedded in these queer organizations and in helping professionals' imaginings of LGBTQ2S+ belonging generally, who define who is deserving of help and care, discussed in Chapter 4.

Ultimately, the goal of this chapter is to reconsider the utility of diversity within queer organizations, communities, and politics, in which queer organizations in Toronto participate. For if inclusion is the answer, how does the desire for diversity further perpetuate white supremacy and settler colonial oppression? And how does the discourse of diversity, as a mechanism non-Indigenous LGBTQ+ helping professionals utilize, require an investment in the white settler colonial nation state? Moreover, how might non-Indigenous LGBTQ+ helping professionals transcend the discourse of diversity within and beyond their queer work by engaging with the realities in which these queer organizations are built? If diversity is the answer, in what ways have queer organizations oriented themselves towards queer liberalism and settler homonationalism? I hope that this series of questions on the use of and orientation towards desiring diversity can spark much-needed conversation and action of non-Indigenous LGBTQ+ helping professionals working within queer organizations (and politics) in Toronto (and Canada) and beyond, so they may work against – in overt and covert ways – the ongoing white racism and settler colonialism that their work often supports and sustains.

The politics and promise of diversity are deeply entrenched within queer organizations themselves and the non-Indigenous LGBTQ+ helping professionals' articulations of who belongs in LGBTQ2S+ spaces. Yet knowing the ways multicultural diversity is utilized by queer organizations only addresses part of the problem; the other facet of queer organizations' culture is the helping professionals' understanding of themselves and the power of their queer helping narratives and motivations of doing queer work. Indeed, the helping paradigm of queer organizations situates the queer helper into power over relationship with those whom they are helping – a relationship that positions queer organizations and the good non-Indigenous LGBTQ+ helping professionals themselves in a powerful relationship.

Chapter Three

"People Like Me?" Non-Indigenous LGBTQ+ Professionals' Helping Motivations

There is no theory that can shield us from the complexity of the gesture of a white middle class woman giving an alcoholic Native homeless man a bowl of soup. It is a gesture that is overdetermined by my history of ancestors who landed in the New World, and great aunts who were missionaries, and great grandparents who were farming folks who moved West and destroyed his linguistic and cultural heritage in order to cover up the theft. We are helping out of this history, not apart from it, and this necessarily troubles the act of helping and thus our identity as helpers. (Rossiter, 2001, n.p.)

Introduction

This chapter situates the helping work done within queer organizations in a larger relationship of white power and privilege: the helper is situated within a longstanding history of paternalism and is trained in how to *help* "Others." Schick (2004) and Ahmed (2000) are critical of helping, specifically the capacity to divide people within the binary of self/Other – a differentiation process that is produced through the relationship between the self (colonizer) the Other (colonized). The self/Other binary is often imagined within the context of international development or mission work, where the enlightened Christian or religious subject brings religious teachings to communities in developing nations in the hopes that they will transform or become civilized (Vaughan, 1991). Paul Willinsky (1998) suggested that coming to know, and ultimately change, the "Other" has evolved out of a history of examination and subservience, which is fuelled by a global colonial project, of which mission work is a part, that attempts to establish, sustain, and maintain differences between the colonizer and the colonized.

As Amy Rossiter (2001) indicated, shown in the epigraph, social work and other helping professions never exist outside of their attachments to and investments in settler colonial history; thus, queer organizations as modern colonial projects are neither removed from this violence nor are they innocent. More specifically, the non-Indigenous LGBTQ+ helping professionals working within queer organizations, given their helping orientation, are placed within a relationship with whomever they help; helping cannot exist outside of historicity. This "helping imperative" – the desire to bring the "Other" into modernity – reinscribes and remakes colonial continuities within the helping professions generally (Heron, 2007). Vowel (2016) notes that the paternalistic logic of the deserving and undeserving Indigenous person continues to be operationalized within the present day by white settler "helpers."

Queer organizations are a function of the European colonial modernity that arose and transpired across the entire globe. This chapter investigates the ways the "helping imperative" is mobilized by non-Indigenous LGBTQ+ helping professionals working within queer organizations in Toronto, suggesting that they are not immune from white-supremacist or settler colonial logics. I consider how non-Indigenous LGBTQ+ helping professionals mobilize white goodness within the helping work they participate in. I address how notions of singular or static understandings of "non-Indigenous LGBTQ+ identity" creep into white helping professionals' understandings of helping as they imagine the service user in need of help to be "like me." Here, the self/Other binary is kept intact, however, it transforms slightly: the imaginings of who is deserving of help rest within the individual helping professional's experiential lexicon.

Being a *Good* Helper

As noted in the introduction, many of the non-Indigenous LGBTQ+ helping professionals interviewed self-identified as white. Given the overrepresentation of white participants and my investment in challenging white supremacy and settler colonialism within the white walls of queer organizations in Toronto, I home in on the ways goodness is constructed. DiAngelo (2018) notes that it is the "progressive" or "woke" white subjects who need to further interrogate their responses to white privilege and complicity since they often have difficulty locating themselves within the problem of systemic white injustice. DiAngelo (2018) notes that, from the vantage point of whites, racism emerges in the form of a dialectic: "racist = bad" and "not racist = good" (p. 72). As Applebaum (2011) argued, evocations of white goodness can often preclude whites from acknowledging and taking responsibility for the white-supremacist structure that they remain deeply tied to and invested in through their whiteness. Within the context of queer organizations in Toronto, non-Indigenous LGBTQ+ helping professionals mobilize a helping relationship, placing them in powerful positions to know the Other, aid in their transformation, and bring them closer to neoliberal civility. As Schick (2014) has suggested, whites "know how to act in ways that illustrate racial dominance; it is their prerogative to make the rules and retain the privilege to transgress them when it suits the project of white supremacy" (p. 99). I extend these authors' discussions of white dominance as *goodness* and argue that, within the context of queer organizations, evocations of whiteness and goodness do very little towards naming and effectively dismantling or even subverting white supremacy and settler colonialism.

Sartia Srivastava (2005) homed in on evocations of white goodness within feminist activist circles in Toronto and addressed how feminists of colour name the actions of white women – who hope to appear as morally good antiracists – as racist. Srivastava (2005) noted that white women's understandings of racism remain deeply individualistic; thus, the naming of white women as racist becomes construed as an attack on their goodness. However, Srivastava (2005) noted, articulations of being good preclude white women from implicating themselves in the white-supremacist system, allowing for routine deflections of acts of racism as doings done by those "bad whites." "The good/bad binary certainly obscures the structural nature of racism and makes it difficult for us [white people] to see or understand [the effects and impacts of white racism]" (DiAngelo, 2018, p. 73). Evocations of white goodness thus allow for white women – or, more broadly, white people – to construct racism as a personality flaw, rather than understanding racism as something that all whites, by their whiteness, routinely sustain and contribute to (Ahmed, 2012; Applebaum, 2011; DiAngelo, 2018; Srivastava, 2005).

White goodness has been theorized by Raneem Azzam (2011) and Daniel Coleman (2006) as being firmly rooted within constructions of white civility. Coleman argued that white civility operates through modalities of neoliberal self-governance, where "the subjects of the civil order discipline their conduct to participate in the civil realm, and they gain or lose legitimacy in an internally striated civil society depending on the degree to which they conform to its ideals" (p. 11). White civility operates within organizations to relocate authority onto white helping professionals generally, as they are required to monitor and discipline themselves through their conduct with BIPOC service users. Moreover,

Azzam (2011) contended that elementary teachers of colour mobilize white civility and are not immune to deploying normative evocations of Canadian nationalism, since within their teaching they continue to invest in multiculturalism and tolerance. As a result, non-Indigenous helping professionals working within queer organizations are not immune to the historical processes of white goodness since they are placed into relationships with the Other by their helping roles (Heron, 2007; Jeffery, 2009).

In theorizing the colonial continuities within NGO development work in parts of Africa, Heron (2007) addressed how white female subjects mobilize the "helping paradigm" within their work. She argued that helping discourses are assembled through white women's bourgeois status, as well as through their sense of entitlement, perceived obligation, and desire to bring African people into modernity. The "helping imperative" is utilized by development workers through their investments in an ongoing white supremacist and colonial project that is veiled by the mission to bring the racialized Other into civility or modernity (Heron, 2007). White development workers utilize the helping imperative as they assume the responsibility to change and significantly increase the quality of life of BIPOC subjects generally. The helping imperative requires helping professionals to know themselves through their intimate encounter with the racialized Other. As a result, helping discourses are mobilized through an encounter with the Other, and this encounter is perceived in the following way: as "romanticizing, identifying with (being 'at one with'), caring for, saving, being seduced by and being transformed through this relationship" with the Other (Heron, 2007, p. 34).

Joseph, a 47-year-old, white, genderqueer person who works as a community-based researcher at a large ASO, and April, a 30-year-old, white, genderqueer person who works as a volunteer at a sexual-health organization, utilize their experiences as HIV/AIDS development workers in Namibia and Malawi as they work in queer organizations in Toronto. Joseph and April shared with me that they gained personal satisfaction by travelling outside of Canada to parts of Africa – a site of racialized desire for white Canadians who want to help care for Africans (Gross, 2015). Joseph discussed how understanding stigma helps them support others and also helps them to engage in social change:

A: It just so happened that those experiences in Malawi crystalized my decision to move away from [the work I was doing] and away from that organization but still [stay] within the HIV sector.

Q: What is your motivation for doing this work?

A: Social Justice. Whether it be queer stigma or HIV stigma or if you are a queer poz [HIV positive] person, you have a couple more layers on there – it is basically about stigma. I guess my personal thing is help people to change, whatever change that is. It could be internal; it could be external – psychological or behavioural. (02/13/13, Transcript 15, p. 4, Toronto, ON)

Joseph's experience with helping others change began when they volunteered as an HIV/AIDS development worker in Malawi. Joseph spoke about how their understandings of stigma can be used to support the service users.

Moreover, April discussed their desire to get involved in the local Toronto community, which emerged out of their experiences doing HIV/AIDS research in Namibia. As they stated:

Q: What brought you to this work?

A: I was living in New York and before that I was in Namibia doing research and a lot of my previous experience around sexual health and HIV had been on an international scale and I had really been looking to make a contribution locally. I found out about this and it met all of the things I wanted to do. So, I wanted to be involved. I always have done a lot of volunteer work and I have interests in sexual health, sexualities, and gender. I felt safe going into the space knowing they were inclusive. (06/05/13, Transcript 40, p. 3, Toronto, ON)

April discussed with me how their experience doing HIV/AIDS work internationally in Namibia provided a deeper context to continue doing sexual-health work locally in Toronto. April's and Joseph's narratives' regarding how their desire to help emerged from development work in Africa, which propels them into a larger transnational helping imperative, one in which is operationalized through the self/Other binary. For Joseph and April, their experiences helping African people propelled them into participating in larger global colonial projects within which they were invited to submit authority as white helpers helping racial Others, devoid of their genderqueer experiences.

Some research participants interviewed mobilized helping narratives through their sexual or gender minority status vis-à-vis their social locations. Discussing the ways white goodness is operationalized in Canadian contexts, Susan Dion (2009) and Thobani (2007) suggest that helping professionals are required to participate in projects of Canadian nation-building that often normalize white settler colonialism. Canada, and by extension the "Canadian" identity of non-Indigenous LGBTQ+ helping professionals I interviewed, is produced not only as good but also as "victimized by outsiders and tolerant of insiders" (Mackey, 2002, 49). As a result, the goodness of whiteness produces itself by normalizing a white settler society that is dependent upon distinctly and yet interrelatedly subordinating BIPOC (Thobani, 2007). Thus, the non-Indigenous LGBTQ+ helping professionals interviewed who partake in helping work can easily normalize and naturalize the effects of white supremacy and settler colonialism – whether occurring through their investments in diversity or discussions of helping LGBTQ2S+ peoples generally.

The helping mobilized by non-Indigenous LGBTQ+ helping professionals can be engaged as a tool to naturalize white settler colonialism through the mobilization of white civility and white goodness. However, as Harjeet Badwall (2013) has theorized, discourses of help mobilized by helping professionals of colour do not necessarily contribute to routine acts of recolonization. Badwall interviewed social workers of colour about their decisions to work within the field of social work and contended that social workers of colour are caught in a double bind whereby in their attempts to address and work towards social justice and antiracism they can reinscribe national projects of white goodness and civility. However, as Badwall described, social workers of colour routinely mobilize the helping imperative differently than their white colleagues, since their helping of Others often "address histories of racism, colonialism and resistance" (p. 185). Badwall's insightful scholarship brought to light the gaps within social work literature around how social workers of colour embody goodness differently than their white colleagues.

Goodness, although historically connected to the white settler missionary project, can also be mobilized by people of colour as a resistance tactic or as a queer-of-colour critique to address the white supremacy and colonialism embedded within Canadian society and within the queer organizations in which they work. The important work of Gordon Pon, Kevin Gosine and Doret Phillips (2011) aligns with Badwall (2013), whereby they note that social workers of colour are invited into the white supremacist imaginary and are simultaneously made to exist outside of the Canadian nation state – as they are required to navigate and encounter subjugation. Moreover, Barbara Waterfall (2002) addressed how Indigenous helping professionals mobilize discourses of help, which may disguise Eurocentrism. Waterfall notes that offering assistance to Others, if done so through colonial mechanisms and orientations, may keep the root of settler colonialism intact – as an unquestioned norm.

Engaging non-Indigenous LGBTQ+ helping professionals' narratives of everyday practices, I consider the ways helping professionals evoke white civility and goodness within their own motivations of helping. I also address how non-Indigenous LGBTQ+ helping professionals of colour actively resist white normativity of queer organizations. It is important to note that, while some of the narratives of people of colour do critique whiteness, their critiques may not necessarily resist the specificities of white settler colonialism that Indigenous peoples, communities, and nations endure and experience.

Motivations for Engaging Queer Work

The narratives below come out of discussions about the research participants' motivations in working within queer organizations. Mark, a 33-year-old, South Asian, queer, cisgender man who works as a peer educator at a youth organization, articulated that his desire to get involved and work within a queer organization came from wanting to reengage queer organizations at the intersection of race, sexuality, and gender.

Q: What is your motivation for doing this work?
A: A lot of people who do this work or are even educators in any way, shape or form are often white women, right? The drop-out rate for especially young men of colour is the highest of any demographic in North America. I believe that people need to see people who they can identify with, talking to them about ... quite frankly teaching them about anything but also talking to them about issues that may very well get spoken about but are not spoken about by people who look like them, or have had experiences like them, so that is a huge reason as to why I do this. (03/15/13, Transcript 26, p. 4, Toronto, ON)

For Mark, the reason for working with queer organizations was to help support and care for other queer people of colour "like him." Similar to Ahmed (2012), Mark takes it upon himself to subvert whiteness normalized within many queer organizations in Toronto and act as a role model for young people of colour. Mark's approach to helping is unlike his white counterparts discussed later and is informed by experiencing and wanting to challenge racism within the queer organization he works for.

Paul, a 28-year-old, white, gay, cisgender man who works as a part-time relief worker at a sexual-health organization, discussed his motivation:

Q: What brought you to this work?
A: Of course, being a gay male, I always knew that there is a higher prevalence of HIV and STIs in our community. When I was finishing up grad school, I felt that I wanted to volunteer. I really wanted to be engaged

in helping people out and I just thought this was a great organization
to do that. (03/23/13/, Transcript 31, p. 4, Toronto, ON)

Paul's involvement stemmed from the aspiration to connect his sexuality to meaningful and rewarding work. Paul's motivation for getting
involved was the desire to support gay men in "our community," a
similar motivation to Cory, a 33-year-old, white, gay, cisgender man
who works as a volunteer at a large organization.

Q: So what brought you to the work that you do?
A: I wanted to participate in a free program and give back to the community. I also joined to gain personal experience, while also giving back
   to my communities, because I had guessed that there might be other
   queers that might need the attention. It was my way of giving back
   my skills to my community. (01/08/13, Transcript 5, p. 4, Toronto, ON)

Cory decided to volunteer for a program that provides accessible
counselling for queer people, and, as he described, he has acquired
newly developed counselling skills that can be potentially useful for
LGBTQ2S+ people. Similarly, Alex, a 50-year-old, white, queer, cisgender man who has worked in various positions and organizations,
discussed with me his motivations for getting involved, particularly
around helping "his community."

Q: Right now ... what are your motivations for volunteering?
A: I want to give back to my community because I realize now more than
   ever that the queer community is my community and I am a proud
   member of it. In my own way I want to help. I started volunteering,
   I went back to school and I am in this whole area quite simply [to] help
   the guy who was where I was. So now I am stepping into my queer
   identity so it is not just about helping the community, it is making a
   statement about myself and it is a way for me to help heal myself, heal
   others and hopefully through my lived experiences and skills that I have
   to help the community. (03/20/13, Transcript 29, p. 5, Toronto, ON)

For Alex, his primary motivation to work within queer organizations is
to heal his own and other queer service users' trauma.

The stories offered by Alex, Cory, and Paul, all of whom identify as
white and cisgender, provide the context to consider how "our/my/
the community" is evoked within the specific context of queer organizations. Although Alex, Cory, and Paul discuss queer organizations
as a site of multiraciality, or diversity, as discussed in Chapter 2, their

evocations of "community" warrant further questioning. As John Paul Catungal (2013) and Giwa and myself (2012) have theorized, particularly within the context of HIV/AIDS organizations in Toronto, evocations of "community" can normalize whiteness by folding the differences of people of colour into queer organizations. The "our/my/the community" evoked by Alex, Cory, and Paul centres them (white, queer/gay, cisgender men) and their desire to help people "like me."

Additionally, Eric, a 39-year-old, white, gay, cisgender man who volunteers at a sexual-health organization, discussed his motivations:

Q: How do Aboriginal peoples fit into your motivations to do this work?
A: I did not get involved because of Aboriginal people. I think it was a motivation because there were gay people there and I identify as gay so I wanted to help out the gay community so that was a motivation, but not so much for Aboriginal peoples. It was cool because there were Aboriginal people there and I enjoyed them and everything. (03/29/13, Transcript 33, p. 11, Toronto, ON)

In addition to the previous narrative of "our/my/the community," I mention Eric's discussion of the service users he imagines in the organization he works at to provide additional context. As Eric discussed with me: "there are a lot of people who are there that are Aboriginal too. I do not think any of them are gay or have identified as gay" (03/29/13, Transcript 33, p. 7, Toronto, ON). Eric's narrative illustrates how Indigenous peoples were not necessarily part of his motivation to volunteer with the queer organization; instead, his initial motivation was to help gay men in "the gay community" he is part of – a community that does imagine Indigenous peoples (Wilson, 1996, 2008). Eric pointed out that, although Indigenous peoples are very much present within the queer organization, they do not fit into his motivations, simply because they are not or have not self-identified as "gay." Although Eric was happy to help and support Indigenous peoples he came into contact with, his overall motivation for getting involved centres gay men – like himself.

Within the particular context of queer organizations in Toronto, non-Indigenous LGBTQ+ research participants spoke about being motivated to get involved as a way to provide "the/our/my community" with assistance and support. Although the research participants indicated their awareness of Toronto as a multiracial or "diverse" city where BIPOC are accessing queer organizations, it is clear that the supposed subject that requires help remains connected to research participants' understandings of being a gender or sexual minority, which is made to matter through the queer organizations' investments in gender and sexuality. For Mark, his involvement in queer organizations occurred so that the normatively white representation of gender and sexuality would be challenged and compromised. Thus, the helping work done by white LGBTQ+ helping professionals within queer organizations can easily reinforce the normatively white construction of a singular LGBTQ2S+ community, further producing white LGBTQ+ service users as deserving of help and care. In order to get a full picture of helping professionals' investments in white settler colonialism, I turn now to a discussion of how goodness is mobilized by helping professionals.

Being and Feeling Good

The narratives offered by the research participants depict how non-Indigenous LGBTQ+ helping professionals easily evoke goodness, which, in effect, can ensure that whiteness remains normalized within queer organizations. As already mentioned, helping professionals, under their helping role, cannot exist outside of history and may be complicit in sustaining white supremacy and settler colonialism. Below, I illustrate how non-Indigenous LGBTQ+ helping professionals offer narratives of goodness as a way to disconnect and deflect their ties to larger projects of nation-building and the ongoing naturalization of white supremacy and settler colonialism. When non-Indigenous LGBTQ+ helping professionals only recognize their actions as good, they can easily avoid considering white supremacy and settler colonialism as being firmly engrained within their own helping orientations and queer organizations generally.

For example, Ronald, a 32-year-old, white, gay, cisgender man who volunteers at a few queer organizations in Toronto, discussed why he started volunteering:

Q: What is your motivation for doing this work?
A: My main motivation is to basically help people. I had such an easy time. I have a very supportive family and friends, and my coming out process was super easy. My being openly gay has been really easy. It really felt like I wanted to pay that forward. It felt like I was in a position where I feel really good about the way I am and I feel really excited about what I am. I feel like being somehow an Other is such a gift and I just wanted to help other people see that. There is a lot of inner turmoil when it comes to sexual orientation. Also, I cannot deny the reward that I get internally from feeling I am doing good work. It makes me feel good and every time I tell someone they tell me "oh, that is so great that you do that." That also makes me feel good. (02/09/13, Transcript 14, p. 4, Toronto, ON)

Ronald's motivations to work within a queer organization stemmed from a desire to extend his positive experiences outward to other LGBTQ2S+ peoples who might not have had such a positive experience "coming out." Ronald's story provides the context to consider how the helping work he does is predicated on his own experiences of marginalization, which he can transcend and feel good about when helping Others whose lives have yet to "get better." Ronald's understanding of gayness as Other is embedded within his whiteness as a white, gay, cisgender man who foresees gay Otherness to be disconnected from other interlocking systems of oppression. As a result, the gay Otherness Ronald evokes as a primary motivator for his helping is a white understanding of gayness as Other insofar as he equates being an Other with the Otherness of any other Other that he might encounter. Moreover, he does this without noticing the power differentials between them, the queer organization, or the capacity for white gayness to Other another Other.

Additionally, Brett, a 31-year-old, white, genderqueer person who works as a part-time relief worker at a sexual health organization, discussed their experiences working at an organization and their desire to transcend HIV/AIDS stigma within their helping professional role.

Q: What are your motivations for doing the work?

A: I find it incredibly rewarding work mostly because I dealt with my shit around HIV. I am not afraid of it. I really relish the opportunity to be able to talk to people about something they never really get to talk about with anyone else. I do not think any old counsellor would decatastrify [sic] sexual health and HIV. It is really nice to be able to make a space for someone that did not necessarily exist for them, but is like safe and accommodating and supportive. So, I love doing that. (04/30/13, Transcript 38, p. 6, Toronto, ON)

Brett's narrative offers a slightly different approach to white queer goodness insofar as they take it upon themself, as their moral duty, to support marginalized service users around their sexual health – this goal is also supported through larger biopolitical efforts to reduce the spread of HIV and other STIs in Toronto. Although Brett spoke about their desire to help in a "non-judgmental way," they also illustrated that the work they do informs their understanding of the self. This helping story connects to Applebaum's (2011) and DiAngelo's (2018) theorization of white goodness, where whites disconnect themselves and their perceived good intentions from larger structures of white supremacy, in which queer organizations are situated. As a result, feeling good about helping Others is directly tied to Brett's own embodied whiteness and imaginings of queerness.

Cassandra, a 29-year-old, white, lesbian, cisgender woman who works as an addictions counsellor at a large mental health organization, also discussed her desire to help the "LGBTQ2S+ community."

Q: What is your motivation for doing this work?
A: I feel that being able to provide a space where I am genuinely able to care about them and follow them through this journey of recovery is quite a privilege. So, I do this work because I really like it. I really enjoy working with the clients. I think we are making a difference in terms of providing the service in general. I think it is its own piece of advocacy, and carving out a space for addictions work is pretty cool and innovative. I think there is a lot of [sic] opportunities in this work to, kind of, on many different levels to help people individually, and to help our community as a whole, and to help our community and other [helping professionals] learn how to work with our community. (02/28/13, Transcript 18, p. 7, Toronto, ON)

Cassandra's narrative links to the helping narratives offered, which evoke "the/our/my community," whereby difference is folded into queer organizations to naturalize the space as normatively white. Here, white goodness is evoked in her desire to help service users accessing substance-use treatment, with the ultimate biopolitical goal, similar to Brett, of reducing harm. As a result, Cassandra's story points to the neoliberal machinery of queer organizations, since this version of help when mobilized presumes that LGBTQ2S+ service users who are using substances can change and (are willing to) reintegrate into society. If service users can embody this particular version of "service user subjectivity," Cassandra can see herself as doing good work. Cassandra's narrative provides an opportunity to consider how white settler goodness manifests in such attempts to bring service users into civil modernity, which requires them to ultimately help themselves and integrate themselves within the contemporary white settler society.

Jett, a 49-year-old, white, gay, cisgender man who works as an addictions counsellor at a large mental-health organization, works at the same organization as Cassandra and discussed the pleasure that he experiences when he can help service users transcend their addiction by making positive changes in their life.

Q: Right now, what are your motivations for doing the work that you do?
A: It is about helping people. It can be a high stress job and there are lots of people who are difficult to deal with or who are so marginalized or are affected by so many different problems. It can feel really overwhelming.

But the reality is we do help lots of people and that is a wonderful sort of thing to be part of. You go from a place where they are in a lot of difficulty, trouble and experiencing a lack of understanding to getting them to a place where they can make connections and make all kinds of changes that they felt were not possible and come out the other side. It gives me tons of pleasure to say goodbye to clients who have done a ton of good work and who are in a really strong position in their lives. I run into people at the gym, or on Church Street, who I have worked with in the past and they are often looking healthy. Sometimes people confide into [sic] me and let me know they are still doing really well and it is great to be part of that. I like talking to people I work with. They are all kinds of interesting people and that continues to give me lots of interest and pleasure. (03/19/13, Transcript 28, p. 4, Toronto, ON)

Jett's narrative connects to Cassandra's around the neoliberalization of queer organizations, where the rhetoric of white goodness is mobilized when helping professionals feel good about the helping work they do. Both Jett and Cassandra feel good when service users leave the program once they can reintegrate into the white settler society. For Jett, this experience induces pleasure, when he hears of and sees former service users who have been able to care for themselves and remain (or appear to remain) sober. Notably, Jett's narrative outlines what many helping professionals are expected to do: good helping professionals are ones that can support the most marginalized into being able to help themselves – in a sense, to no longer need or require organizations since they can reintegrate into and contribute to the larger white settler society.

Although white helping professionals mobilize their goodness in ways that reify and normalize the whiteness of queer organizations, it is equally important to consider how goodness is employed by LGBTQ+ helping professionals of colour. As Badwall (2013) argued, helping professionals of colour mobilize goodness as a way to challenge the normative whiteness of organizations. Lisa, a 49-year-old, mixed-race, cisgender lesbian who works as a newcomer-service coordinator at a large organization, shared a story of goodness that is enacted through her ability to seek support surrounding her settlement and her subsequent personal satisfaction found in helping others through their settlement process.

Q: What is your motivation for doing this work?
A: I have to admit that during the time that I have worked in Canada it has worked for me too in my own settlement process. It has been great

therapy with me also in my own quest for settlement in Canada. It has created a community for me too. I personally feel it has been very fulfilling on a professional level. I think I have managed to excel at doing this because I enjoy it so incredibly much. It is incredibly rewarding. (01/15/13, Transcript 9, p. 7, Toronto, ON)

Lisa's commitment to her work around the issues LGBTQ+ immigrants and/or people of colour experience as they connect to settlement in Canada has contributed to her personally by creating community and professionally by helping other service users "like her" in navigating the immigration system in Ontario, Canada. The work that Lisa does requires her as an LGBTQ+ immigrant and/or person of colour to consciously challenge the white supremacy and colonialism that refugees experience when trying to traverse the immigration system in Canada. For Lisa, her goodness is mobilized through her capacity to aid other LGBTQ+ immigrants and/or people of colour in navigating the immigration system that scrutinizes their refugee claims because they are seen as not being queer enough.

As Emily, a 52-year-old, white, lesbian, cisgender woman who works at the same queer organization as Lisa as the director of programs, suggested: "this organization has become the first place [for queer refugees] to stop and get a letter or acknowledgement that they are queer" (12/23/12, Transcript 2, p. 5, Toronto, ON). The immigration system in Canada has set up exclusionary criteria for refugee claimants in order for them to be read as queer. To be able to justify their refugee status, claimants must submit themselves to routine surveillance and document how their sexuality or gender and the violence they do (or might) experience as a result of their sexuality or gender impacts their safety and their need to settle in Canada. Thus, Lisa's version of goodness involves attempts to work within the confines of queer organizations, and indeed the immigration system in Canada, to provide support for and to help other refugee claimants navigate the harsh and often violent realities of white supremacy and (settler) colonialism that impede on their daily life – since failing to be read as queer can result in a refugee claimant's deportation. This concept of being "queer enough," linked with the white settler colonial system of immigration, means that whether she believes she is doing good or not, Lisa is inextricably part of a queer organization that both inflicts violence upon and acts to support LGBTQ+ immigrants and/or people of colour.

Skyler, a 25-year-old, mixed-race, genderqueer person who works at the same queer organization as Lisa as a part-time administrator, spoke of their experience with working to subvert the normatively white confines within the organization they work at.

Q: What is your motivation for doing this work?

A: I have no motivations. I am pretty good at this job because I am the only one who is super friendly to all the clients who come in here no matter what they look like. I am friendly to them. I make sure they are welcomed and warmed. I cannot really leave to do anything with the managers, but I can work with the people who walk in who need support. I can work under this regime to create space for all. Not just rich white gay men who support us [the organization] with dollars. (01/09/13, Transcript 7, p. 4, Toronto, ON)

Skyler's story points to the constraints that are placed on helping professionals and their attempts to subvert the white-supremacist and settler colonial confines of queer organizations. Similar to how Catungal (2013) discussed how large ASOs reinscribe white, gay male dominance, Skyler called attention to the structural limitations of their queer organization, particularly to the investments made in white gayness, as white, gay, cisgender males can support the organization financially. Skyler discussed taking every opportunity to challenge the normativity of whiteness within their organization and trying to make the working environment more inclusive by being welcoming of difference. However, Skyler's narrative provides an opportunity to consider the possibilities in engaging in resistance being mobilized by LGBTQ+ people of colour in queer organizations when they do not always have the authority or decision-making power – what Hyde (2018) calls "low-power actors."

Similar to Skyler, Alex, a 50-year-old, white, queer, cisgender man who has worked in various positions and organizations, shared a narrative in which he named the organization as a whole as normatively white.

Q: You talked a little bit about who the service users were at [the organization], did you want to expand at all on that?

A: One of the reasons I love the group I am co-facilitating right now is that there is [sic] six people and four of them are not Caucasian which I find at this organization is unusual. I love it because in my training at this organization … the volunteers were predominantly white and probably the majority of them were male. Most of the folks working, volunteering and who are clients seem to be white. So, I just like the diversity because to me it reflects the community and it reflects the city. (03/20/13, Transcript 29, p. 6, Toronto, ON)

The diversity within his support group shifted Alex's perception of who belongs at the organization by troubling the whiteness associated with the organization. While Alex is critical of the organization's white-ness, he uses diversity as a way to associate difference with the bodies that enter the organization, which ultimately sustains the queer space as white. As a result, although Alex can feel good about the work that he is doing with marginalized service users who are "not Caucasian," he reinscribes white goodness even as he mobilizes his critique.

While white goodness operates within everyday moments within queer organizations, it also manifests in non-Indigenous LGBTQ+ helping professionals' articulations of what a good helping profes-sional should do. As Kate, a 25-year-old, white, bisexual/queer, cisgen-der woman who works as a women's sexual-health coordinator at a sexual-health organization, argued, critique for critique's sake does not engage antiracist action within the context of queer organizations. Kate discussed how helping professionals "talk the talk" while noting that this talk can preclude any structural change.

Q: What is an example of someone saying "oh my gosh my privilege"?
A: I think that helping professionals get good at the talk, right. For example, I always say I am acknowledging my privilege, but I am left asking:
   but then what? I say all of this feeling guilty of that myself, just to be
   clear. I know that a bad habit of mine that I fall into is getting immobi-
   lized by my concern about the ways I might enact racism so that I just
   do not do anything, that I do not engage with communities of colour,
   that I do not engage at all. Which I think is a problematic dynamic. It
   is so much easier to pick on things than it is to actually suggest alter-
   natives or new ways of practicing within the work that we do. I think
   that sometimes people say that and they mean, "if you do not have
   anything nice to say, then do not say it at all." From my experience,
   there is a lot of talk and not a lot of action. (03/01/13, Transcript 19,
   p. 34, Toronto, ON)

Kate discussed how non-Indigenous LGBTQ+ helping professionals "get good at the talk" but fail to act in transformative ways, which can often reinscribe their whiteness. Kate suggested that helping profes-sionals need to move beyond critique within their work by proposing new ways of practicing as one way to engage with everyday forms of racism. Kate's narrative points to how cause-and-effect thinking is sustained within queer organizations by requiring tangible and deliv-erable outcomes that may not necessarily engage in or effectively do antiracist work (DiAngelo, 2018) or anticolonial work (Cannon, 2012). Kate's narrative also connects to Jeffery's (2005) discussion of good anti-racist social workers and their desire for prescriptive steps to address racism, placing her in a complex relationship with queer organizations whereby white goodness is enacted in calls for action that reify organizational institutions. Kate's narrative also connects to the work of Lensmire et al. (2013) and DiAngelo (2018) insofar as they argued that white-privilege talk alone can reinscribe white supremacy in centring the learning of the individual white subject since no real antiracist action occurs. Moreover, given the calls to action of Cannon (2012) and Indigenous activists related to the TRC and missing and murdered Indigenous women, girls, and 2-Spirit people noted in the introduction, Kate's discussion of inaction and "the talk" is also related to anticolonial work to unearth the effects and impacts of white settler colonialism in Indigenous peoples' lives, communities, and nations (Million, 2013; Regan, 2010).

Mobilizing what Kate called "the talk," Nicole, a 46-year-old, white, queer, cisgender woman who works as a program coordinator at a youth organization, discussed the need to address and name one's white privilege by looking inward and becoming conscious of one's embodiment.

Q: Do you experience challenges or obstacles?
A: Yes. [laughs]

Q: What would be some of those?
A: I question myself regularly. This is being really transparent, is being white, middle aged now, middle class. I carry privilege and I know that I do good work. I know that I am committed to this work and I know where I have come from. But I also acknowledge and feel some pressure around that. Maybe I should step aside and make space for someone else. Some of the challenges relate to not being able to do enough and not really knowing why we are not doing enough. I want to truly respond to the needs of young people and communities whether it is the Black community or First Nations youth, and knowing that there might be people from those communities who are looking and going: "so, most of your staff are white, how are you ever going to deal with that if you do not change that?" We have been working on trying to change that. However, that is all tied up with, "I have been here a long time." I am conscious of that and try to lead with being comfortable with my discomfort around that and work through it rather than just feel guilty because it is not helpful. (03/13/13, Transcript 25, p. 4, Toronto, ON)

Nicole's story illuminates the problems that occur when one's white privilege is named. However, centring one's learning on white privilege can obscure the structural realities (e.g., white supremacy) within which one benefits (Ahmed, 2012; DiAngelo, 2018; Lensmire et al., 2013). Although Nicole brought up the need to embrace discomfort, her story can reinscribe her white dominance as she attempts to critique her organization and simultaneously seems to situate herself as knowing or helping (Ahmed, 2012; Applebaum, 2011). The naming of one's white privilege cannot be the only actionable antiracist or anticolonial action helping professionals mobilize, since doing so can prohibit action-oriented steps, as Kate mentions, which can effectively subvert and even challenge systems of white supremacy and settler colonialism.

Although Thomas, a 25-year-old, white, gay, cisgender man who works as a volunteer at a large ASO, did not name his white privilege, he discussed how he utilizes his friendships with Indigenous peoples as a way to remain aware of Indigenous issues and bring this awareness into the work he does.

Q: Are there any additional issues that need to be raised as part of this research?

A: Personally, I have two [Aboriginal] friends who do not live on reserves. I have learned so much [from them]. I am empathetic. One of my friends is Metis and the other one is Ojibway. From them, I have been more sensitive and it has informed my volunteer work. It is a shame that it has not happened with the other people I volunteer with. (12/12/12, Transcript 1, p. 8, Toronto, ON)

Thomas's narrative illustrates that he remains aware of Indigenous content and contexts due to his relationships with two Indigenous friends. Thomas' narrative illuminates how the self/Other binary – coming to know the self concerning another Other – remains central to how he understands his role as a helping professional. Thomas' story connects to Alison Jones's (1999) work on the removal of Pakeha (white) students from the same learning spaces as that of the Maori and Pacific Islander when the Pakeha students saw themselves as entitled to "learn from the Other." Thomas' white settler goodness is evoked in him requiring the Indigenous Other (his friends) to be the one enlightening him.

Candy, a 27-year-old, South Asian, genderqueer person who works as a student intern at a large not-for-profit organization, discussed how notions of solidarity can easily reinscribe settler dominance within organizational contexts.

Q: What do you mean by appropriative?

A: I find it often is on the good person list. You know, that like to be understood a good person is you recycle, you buy free trade, free range beef, and then Indigenous solidarity is just one of the things that you do. I think there are plenty of people who are really engaged in these things and that is super. But I also think that it can be like any other anti-racist politic like wearing a pin or a patch and that is your politic. But the Indigenous piece, as you are finding is the hot spot for people. What does [it] mean to be Canadian? "You need to shut the fuck up about that." And that is, that is the easiest thing for white queers to let go of. (01/15/13, Transcript 8, p. 3, Toronto, ON)

Candy called out the complicity of white LGBTQ+ people generally in Toronto queer communities who want to be read as good by simply including Indigeneity among other solidarity endeavours. Candy importantly noted that Indigenous solidarity can be very essentializing, similar to other alliance politics that will be discussed in Chapter 5, and that its significance can be trivialized. Such evocations of Indigenous solidarity within white LGBTQ+ people's notions of goodness act to centre whiteness and settler colonialism and thereby disavow anticolonial action that is central to Indigenous self-determination and resurgence. Therefore, the naming of Indigenous solidarity does not require action, just as Candy described, and does almost nothing, as its naming alone reinscribes white settler colonialism in such attempts to appear good.

Brett, a 31-year-old, white, genderqueer person who works as a part-time relief worker at a sexual-health organization, discussed their understandings of how decolonization informs the work they do.

Q: How do Aboriginal peoples fit into your motivations to do the work that you do?

A: As a white person who does not have any Aboriginal ancestry, words like solidarity sound really nice but are not necessarily appropriate. One thing I would reflect on is some of how I conceive parallel discourses around decolonization as especially for queer Aboriginal people. Really setting a standard and having some really strong leaders who have taught me a lot about the way the world works and about the way colonialism works and how we can think about decolonizing. I am really committed to this idea of acknowledging colonialism. If there is a problem or something that is not good in my life I cannot look away from it and pretend it is not there. I have to fully invest myself in understanding and having a position on it or a place in that rather than avoiding it, right. So in terms of Aboriginal peoples' rights and activism, I do as much as I can to learn, to listen, to speak when appropriate and to shut up when not appropriate. (04/30/13, Transcript 38, p. 10, Toronto, ON)

Brett's narrative attempts to engage with Candy's cautioning of Indigenous solidarity politics within queer organizations and communities in Toronto. Brett spoke about how mentors of theirs and leaders, similar to Thomas, in the community have taught them about colonialism and decolonization, stating that they are committed to acknowledging colonialism and learning about Indigenous peoples in Canada. Here, Brett's narrative provides the context to consider how queer helping professionals' experiences can provide an opportunity to take Indigenous decolonization seriously. Although Brett has taken active steps in acknowledging how white power and privilege intersect with colonialism, their narrative points to difficulty in considering how their version of decolonization can easily connect to an analytic of settler colonialism and white supremacy of which they and their work are a part.

Conclusion

As some non-Indigenous LGBTQ+ helping professionals articulated, they remain deeply invested in helping people "like me" within queer organizations so that they can help support "the/our/my community." These investments articulate complex relationships with queer organizations that are mandated to support divergent LGBTQ2S+ people. The white research participants' narratives of helping illustrate how feeling – and wanting to be read as – good can easily reinscribe and normalize whiteness. Good intentions of the white participants can easily reinscribe white dominance even when the institution's whiteness is being critiqued. Moreover, David and Lisa offer an opportunity to consider the ways queers of colour are working within normatively white queer organizations in Toronto and are actively helping Others – yet their mobilization of helping is different from that of their white counterparts. This chapter utilized the motivation narratives of non-Indigenous LGBTQ+ helping professionals to understand how goodness and helping are negotiated when "like me" is centred, an act that can erase BIPOC and centre whiteness by outwardly producing oneself as good.

In opposition to the motivations and explanations of queer helping work, in Chapter 4 I explore the ways non-Indigenous LGBTQ+ helping professionals imagine Indigenous peoples within their respective queer organizations. These imaginings are situated within larger white settler colonial logics of erasure that associate Indigenous peoples, communities, and nations as unworthy of care – they are produced as necropolitical subjects who should be already dead and, consequently, disassociated from queerness as an abject identity and political category.

Chapter Four

Necropolitical Care: The Practice of Indigenous Exclusion

The colonial undertaking left behind it only the remainders of the [Indigenous] population that it has, for that matter, hastened to confine to enclaves. By restricting occasions for meeting and contact between settlers and the subjugated, both groups were set at a maximal distance – a prior condition for the banalizing of indifference ... conquest and colonial occupation demanded not only an extraordinary aptitude for indifference but also normdefying capacities to perform properly repugnant acts. (Mbembe, 2019, p. 127)

Introduction

Helping professionals often use *care* and *caring* interchangeably. They, as part of their role and responsibilities, are required to care for populations that their organizations name and support. As Kelly (2016) argues "care and help are intricately interwoven with violence, oppression, and harm" (p. 35). Yet while there is truth to the ways care enters into helping professionals' helping ethos, the care that they mobilize is often "rooted in specific situated power dynamics" (Kelly, 2016, p. 35) that emerge from social, political, and cultural contexts. Critically analysing the ways care or caring is mobilized within queer organizations, this chapter addresses the ways non-Indigenous LGBTQ+ helping professionals reproduce white settler colonialism within their helping practices. White settler colonialism – deeply rooted in all helping professions in Canada – impacts the politics and practices of care evoked by non-Indigenous LGBTQ+ helping professionals. As such, the care mobilized by non-Indigenous LGBTQ+ helping professionals is situated within a logic of erasure – whereby BIPOC are often erased from queer spaces and queer belonging.

White settler colonialism, a mechanism that rests upon the erasure of Indigenous peoples, is produced through non-Indigenous LGBTQ+ helping professionals' narratives of exclusion. Such narratives of exclusion are amplified by the rhetoric of neoliberal queer politics that emphasize inclusion under the state (e.g., gay and lesbians can legally marry), explained in detail in Chapter 2. Consequently, the imaged and very real inclusion of LGBTQ2S+ peoples and communities requires Indigenous peoples and Indigeneity to be evicted from queer spaces of belonging and worth, including queer organizations. As a result, the practice of inclusion within Toronto's queer organizations requires white settler colonialism to function by normalizing a "politics of care" – that is, some lives become liveable and worth caring for, while others become marked as degenerate and, as a result, are worth letting die. This politics of care becomes entrenched within queer organizations and the practices of non-Indigenous LGBTQ+ helping professionals, shown in their articulations of why Indigenous peoples utilize the services at their respective organizations and, more specifically, the limits placed upon Indigenous peoples' accessing services.

The Bio- and Necropolitical Realities of (Queer) Organizations

Million's (2013) ground-breaking research on contemporary helping professions in Canada and the United States, health and healing, and Indigenous self-determination provides the necessary critique with which to engage with queer organizations in Canada. Million has argued that contemporary helping professions, which have been set up to support and help, among others, Indigenous peoples, are based on their injury and have made an industry out of their trauma. As Piepzna-Samarasinha (2018) notes, many marginalized disabled people evade the care they desperately need, since accepting care means accepting control over their bodies and minds. The caring industry, which Kelly (2016) argues is both undervalued and feminized work, often does a disservice to Indigenous peoples, communities, and nations, since the caring work done by non-Indigenous peoples is situated within the bio-politics of settler colonialism: "a historical and present condition and method of all such power" of the "biopolitical state, regimes of global governance, and the war on terror" (Morgensen, 2011a, p. 54). As such, caring work is rarely benevolent as discussed in Chapter 3; rather, helping, and the care one receives or does not, is situated within a transnational nexus of white settler colonialism.

To theorize the biopolitics of settler colonialism, Morgensen utilizes the foundational work of Micheal Foucault (1978) to highlight how biopolitics – "power over life" (p. 139) – is directly tied to historical and contemporary realities in which Indigenous peoples are subjugated to ongoing violence, erasure, and displacement. The theorization of the biopolitics of settler colonialism is also operationalized within queer organizations, since helping professionals continue to normalize Indigenous erasure, as discussed in Chapter 5. Helping professionals' contribution to the politics of care is equally important to analyse in order to interrogate often overlooked, violent, day-to-day practices. These mundane practices, what Mark Rifkin (2013) calls *quotidian*, must be engaged to highlight how the everyday workings of white settler life contribute to the consumption of and investment in white settler colonialism. Thus, looking at the origins of theorizing biopolitics can assist in understanding why and how particular populations are marked as deserving of care.

Foucault (1978) theorized the concept of *biopolitics*, which many scholars utilize to make sense of how discourse shapes human sexuality and the body. Foucault's work on biopolitics considers how bodies become disciplined and populations controlled – emphasizing the dynamics between individual agency and the structural forces in which individuals are situated. For Foucault, the life of the individual becomes disciplined, regulated, and monitored (Nguyen, 2010). Thus, the concept of biopolitics becomes useful insofar as the life of an individual is attributed to their value and thus deemed sufficiently worthy of life and care. In the context of this book, the bodies of biopolitics that are made to matter are Indigenous peoples who utilize – or try to utilize – LGBTQ2S+ services and programs, as well as queer organizations. In light of this concept of "managing life" and the care of the larger population, helping professionals are thus placed in powerful positions – similarly to that of the sovereign of which Foucault (1978) theorized – to support and care for those service users who are deemed deserving of life and care – a project of modernity and neoliberal civility. Thus, the management of difference, in the context of queer organizations, is to bring service users marked as life, and thus worthy of care into modernity. Care, then, is also wrapped up in white LGBTQ+ service providers understandings of "the/our/my community" discussed in Chapter 3 into a state of normalcy – they too, can become productive, self-sufficient, neoliberal Canadian citizens.

Consequently, however, service users who are disconnected from life are deemed unworthy of support and care – in essence, helping professionals shared with me that Indigenous peoples are often too difficult to care for. This unworthiness of life is explored by Achille Mbembe (2003), who utilizes Foucault's (1978) theorization of biopolitics by

offering the concept of *necropolitics* – the production of a people or population as already dead. Mbembe looks to the site of the plantation,
which allowed white enslavers to understand enslaved Black peoples
and their existences as already dead. By "already dead" Mbembe is
referring to the disposability of Black peoples and populations from
life as we know it – or their possibility of rehabilitation – they are rendered unworthy of life. Utilizing Mbembe's scholarship to examine the
death of Indigenous men in police custody, Razack (2015) noted that
the necropolitical construction of Indigenous peoples produces them as
being unworthy of help or intervention. Razack found that white settler police officers would often ignore Indigenous men asking for help
as they were supposed to be already dead – their lives are not worth
living.

In conjunction with Razack, Talaga (2017) documents seven Indigenous youth who went missing in Thunder Bay, Ontario. When parents or guardians were frightened and concerned, they would call the
local police unit only to be repeatedly told: "'There are no leads,' or
other comments like, 'He is just out there partying.' ... the Thunder Bay
Police did not take [Indigenous peoples] calls seriously" (p. 113). There
is historical and contemporary mistrust in the Canadian government
and all of its attending forces given the advent of residential schools,
the 60s scoop, and other systemic and bureaucratic inequalities, including police violence. In the case of Jethro Anderson going missing, it
took the local police unit six days to put together a missing-person
investigation. Talaga's work provides yet another example of the work
of necropolitics producing Indigenous peoples as unworthy of life or
care; in conjunction with calls to action regarding missing and murdered Indigenous women, girls, and LGBTQ2S+ people, the power of
white settler colonialism further sediments the popular perception that
Indigenous peoples generally are abject.

Looking to the media coverage of Indigenous peoples' activism surrounding the "Caledonia crisis" and Indigenous activism of 1492 Land-
Back Lane in 2020 (Kennedy, 2020) – the construction and development
of housing complexes on Indigenous peoples' lands – I have shown
how white settlers use disability or mad tropes, such as wacko, as
one way to mark Indigenous peoples and nations as "pathological" –
as being in a perpetual state of abnormalcy (Greensmith, 2012). I highlighted how the imbricated logics of settler colonialism and ableism
(or madness) marked the activism of Indigenous peoples as "out of
the ordinary," and thus, Indigenous peoples were constructed as "less-
than-human," rationalizing their routine erasure – in Six Nations and
elsewhere in Canada – delegitimizing their calls for decolonization,

self-determination, and sovereignty (Greensmith, 2012). Thus, the theorization of biopolitics and necropolitics with that of white settler colonialism further produces Indigenous peoples, communities, and nations as "deficits," "problems," and/or "pathological" who ultimately require correction, assimilation, and/or extermination.

John's narrative explicitly connects to the necropolitical construction of Indigenous peoples, whereby his story highlights how Indigenous trans peoples are rendered disposable. Specifically sharing a story when working as a case manager, John, a 54-year-old, white, gay, cisgender man who has worked in various positions and organizations, spoke with me about a particular Indigenous service user he remembered supporting.

> I remember working with an Aboriginal person who was trans-identified, but they did not pass as a woman in any way. At the time, they were experiencing psychotic episodes and I could only infer that they had a really complex and difficult life of incarceration and involvement in mental health services. They were living in a dumpster at the time, and due to lack of access to hygiene facilities, I tried really hard to spend time in a room with them. I almost threw up all the time. As a result of their mental health, they threatened harm and violence toward others. They were one of the most vulnerable marginalized people that I have ever worked with and that was at [organization name removed] that has a reputation for being a nice white middle class organization with lots of nice white middle class people that access services. This person was certainty someone whose life was very different. (03/21/13, Transcript 30, p. 12, Toronto, ON)

John shares a story where he remembered a psychiatrized or mad Indigenous trans person within a "nice white middle class [queer] organization." John uses pathologizing language, such as "experiencing psychotic episodes," as a way to make sense of the Indigenous, trans service user's experiences of trauma; after all, this Indigenous service user was perceived to be unable to take care of themselves, and, to their demise, was unable to pass as female. As such, this particular story illuminates John's goodness in that, despite the Indigenous service user's shortcomings and the constraints placed upon John (and his queer organization), he was able to provide this Indigenous person with "adequate" care, from his perspective. Here, white settler goodness operates within John's narrative to sustain the necropolitical construction of Indigenous peoples as "problems" through the inability of white LGBTQ+ helping professionals to recognize Indigenous peoples' experiences of multigenerational trauma outside of a white settler imaginary.

Biopolitical and necropolitical logics – determining who is deserving of care – continue to infiltrate contemporary queer organizations, which are heavily influenced by biomedical and psychiatric regimes. The power of these institutions and schools of thought habitually disregard how the colonial trauma experienced by Indigenous peoples is a consequence of ongoing white settler colonialism – neglect, mistreatment, and genocide – in Canada. Thus, the neoliberal framing of "correcting" Indigenous peoples' problems turns their trauma and its consequences into an individual "problem" of the mind or an outcome of one's life circumstances. But, as Million (2013) argued, the trauma that Indigenous peoples experience must be connected to contemporary white settler colonial life – of which queer organizations are a part. This is of particular importance since, within the context of queer organizations in Toronto, sexuality and gender become primary causes of concern while leaving other axes of oppression (e.g., [settler] colonialism) disconnected or at best minimized. As Million argued, Indigenous peoples may not require biomedical or psychiatric supports to heal from their historical and colonial wounds. Importantly, Million has cautioned those who mobilize the white settler colonial modalities of care to consider how Indigenous peoples are recolonized by mainstream, white-normed biomedical and psychiatric regimes. In decentring white settler colonial care and intervention, Indigenous communities can centre their forms of decolonization, sovereignty, and self-determination – since Indigenous healing requires community because the entire nation is impacted and connected.

While many of the supports and services available to Indigenous peoples within queer organizations can dismiss or downplay the effects of white settler colonialism in their lives, alcohol treatment programs (e.g., Alcoholics Anonymous) often require its participants to abstain from any form of substance use. Moreover, these types of alcohol treatment plans are based on a modernist and settler colonial paradigm where participants are required to invest in a higher being to become, and hopefully remain, sober. Richard Thatcher (2004) addressed the particularities of substance-use treatments within Indigenous communities and illustrated that alcohol treatment programs often assume that the problem (e.g., alcoholism) is situated within the individual's shortcomings. The individualistic understanding of alcoholism – one can abstain from alcohol use – fuels the perception that Indigenous peoples who consume alcohol are "problems." This framing of alcohol use – that Indigenous peoples are understood as naturally "alcoholic" – fuels the popular understanding that the only way to stop alcoholism within Indigenous communities is to invest in a "disease model" that frames the "problem" as an individual's alcohol "abuse." As Thatcher suggested:

> the firewater complex is not only a set of beliefs about the vulnerability to alcohol of First Nations people, but it also includes a set of informal beliefs that guide the drinking pattern of socially disaffected band members, implicitly justify drunken episodes, and serve as an exclude for drunken comportment. (p. 130)

Thatcher (2004) further argued that, "historically, alcohol treatment programs, similar to care itself, for Indigenous peoples largely gr[ew] out of paternalistic, federal responses to social problems in First Nations ... aimed at alcohol abuse" (p. 352). Focusing only on alcoholism and alcohol consumption does little to address the larger structural realities that make alcohol use an appropriate coping mechanism – with such a mechanism, one might be able to live through Indigenous experiences of loss, trauma, and (cultural) genocide. What needs to be questioned is why these types of interventions, such as alcohol treatment programs, are often devoid of Indigenous peoples' lived realities of white settler colonialism and anti-Native racism. Thus, Thatcher argued that the colonial biomedical discourses embedded within contemporary alcohol treatment programs utilized within the helping professions rely on the construction of Indigenous peoples as "problems," which relocates alcoholism as an individual problem rather than as a consequence of the effects of white settler colonialism.

Evolving out of Thatcher's discussion of alcohol treatments and programs for Indigenous peoples, Amanda's story addresses the need to separate Indigenous substance-use treatment from that of LGBTQ+ programs. Amanda, a 28-year-old, white, queer/lesbian, cisgender woman with Indigenous ancestry who works as a manager at a large mental-health organization, notes:

> Q: How do Aboriginal peoples fit into your motivations in doing this work?
> A: I think that again that is a very highly marginalized population and for me who is not doing the direct clinical work I see more high level information. So what I am seeing is that we are constantly receiving referrals for folks who are identifying non-beverage alcohol as their substance of concern. We do not really see that in the queer service and I think that when we look at the social determinants of health that is such a clear example that the person who is identifying Listerine as an issue versus vodka. There is a huge discrepancy when you look at the population. So I think that there is a huge motivation to work with Aboriginal folks when

you see tangible examples in the ways in which that group is not only marginalized but the way that that marginalization manifests into different concerns that they have. (04/2313, Transcript 35, p. 5, Toronto, ON)

Amanda's role within her queer organization is administrative, and thus she continues to receive referrals from Indigenous-led organizations for Indigenous service users to access LGBTQ+-specific addictions services. Yet, in differentiating the substance-use concerns of Indigenous peoples from those of non-Indigenous LGBTQ+ peoples, Amanda places Indigenous peoples into a category deemed worthy of care, under the auspice of "Aboriginal" addiction programming, insofar as public health deems the consumption of Listerine as harmful. Amanda pointed to the substance-use patterns of Indigenous peoples she encounters and how their specific concerns motivate her care work to reduce Indigenous peoples' overall harm. Amanda's narrative addresses how Indigenous peoples' substance-use concerns become the focal point of helping professionals' care work – often erasing other issues and experiences, specifically (settler) colonialism, for a real and present issue Indigenous peoples are trying to cope with.

Focusing on substance use alone can easily erase the everyday processes and practices of white settler colonialism that Indigenous peoples experience that make substance use an appropriate coping mechanism of choice. Thus, the "deficit" construction of Indigenous peoples as alcoholic is used in Amanda's narrative to suggest that Indigenous peoples with substance-use concerns must access services to be cared for and brought into modernity – they too can achieve neoliberal civility with the help of white settler allies. In connection with Million (2013) and Thatcher's work on Indigenous people's health, white supremacy and settler colonialism must be considered social determinants of health and be addressed when working with Indigenous peoples. Interestingly, within Amanda's story, Indigenous peoples seem to be rendered straight – disconnected from the possibility of benefiting from LGBTQ+ addictions programming and support.

Using Million and Thatcher's work, I argue that attention must be directed towards the white settler colonial structure of contemporary queer organizations. In the pages that follow, I look to the everyday practices of non-Indigenous LGBTQ+ helping professionals to examine how Indigenous peoples become rendered "problems" who ultimately become undeserving of care. The non-Indigenous LGBTQ+ helping professionals I spoke with typically positioned Indigenous peoples outside of the purview of the queer organizations they work within and consequently as not worthy of their care or help. The narratives analysed illustrate how Indigenous peoples are positioned within a "politics of care," often being referred to as "troubled" and/or "pathological," which normalizes the necropolitics of white settler colonialism within the context of queer organizations in Toronto.

The research participants' narratives of Indigeneity intensify the notion that Indigenous peoples are to be treated differently in queer organizations – as unimaginable, unworthy of care, and at times too difficult to care for. These necropolitical logics are normalized within the general culture of queer organizations since they derive from the broader white settler culture; queer organizations' caring goal is to manage and control populations by bringing them into neoliberal civility. Thus, when non-Indigenous LGBTQ+ helping professionals utilize (and normalize) the necropolitical constructions of what Indigenous means – even in forms that are intended as antiracist, anticolonial, or as embracing of Indigenous peoples' diversity – these non-Indigenous LGBTQ+ helping professionals have uniquely individualized historical and contemporary ramifications of white settler colonialism that make such problematic constructions of Indigenous peoples possible. This issue, explored within the context of queer organizations, is rooted in all helping professions, as they attempt to be inclusive of multiracial and multicultural differences and diversity. Yet packed into such claims are the ongoing investments in organizational structures (and the larger white settler society) that rationalize the necropolitical understanding of Indigenous peoples.

Narratives of Indigenous Exclusion

I present here some stories that mark and depict Indigenous peoples differently – constructing them to be outside of white settler rationality and neoliberal models of queer care. In speaking with Jett, a 49-year-old, white, gay, cisgender man who works as an addictions counsellor at a large mental-health organization, he shared with me the kinds of barriers Indigenous peoples face within LGBTQ2S+ communities in Toronto. Packed into Jett's narrative is the simultaneous understanding that Indigenous peoples experience violence and that their experiences of violence are connected to their unwillingness to assimilate into Canada.

Q: In your opinion, is the LGBTQ+ community concerned with people of colour?

A: Yes, perhaps more so than the Aboriginal community. I think Aboriginals are very marginalized, misunderstood, ostracized in lots of ways.

I think lots of people of colour can fit in and maybe be more generally accepted.

Q: Why do you say that?
A: There is a lot of prejudice towards First Nations people. My impression, I guess, in talking to lots of folks, is that people feel that Aboriginal folks do not really want to fit in. They do not really want to assimilate. But that creates challenges for a lot of people who are not sensitive to that. And, who really wants to have to deal with someone who has a lot of, maybe, anger. (03/19/13, Transcript 28, p. 2, Toronto, ON)

Jett's narrative illustrates that he feels people of colour want to assimilate, that some people of colour have assimilated successfully, and that it would be a good idea for people of colour and Indigenous peoples to assimilate. However, within Jett's narrative, the assimilation of people of colour is something that is never named. Jett holds a strong investment in the normalization of white supremacy and settler colonialism as the only modes through which people are allowed to be understood as human.

Jett's story provides a context to consider how whiteness is normalized within LGBTQ2S+ communities and organizations, whereby the mythology that BIPOC are required to assimilate is sustained, as discussed in Chapter 2. Moreover, in this process of thinking through the need for assimilation, we can observe that the ongoing struggles of Indigenous peoples for self-determination and sovereignty are being reduced to the realm of individuality and also seen to be a product of their anger. Rene Linklater (2014) notes that helping professionals who are invested in decolonization must be critical of Western biomedicine and psychiatry more generally as these approaches can cause more trauma as they disengage or minimize the impact of traditional forms of healing in the lives of Indigenous peoples.

Moreover, considering the psychological impact of white colonialism in Indigenous people's lives in Australia, Pat O'Shane (1995) argues,

I recognized the things that happened to the thousands of other Aboriginal families like our family, and I marveled that we weren't all stark, raving mad. I met 'white' people whose experiences of life from first consciousness were of continual affirmation of their being; their self-esteem had never been attacked or questioned in any way; they had no concept of rejection by their families, and the community around them. They were totally confident of their place in society; and they disported themselves with the physical and social demeanour of people who knew nothing of the never-ending quest to know who one is; nothing of the struggle to assert one's existence in the world. (p. 153)

O'Shane's narrative highlights the ways Indigenous peoples experience violence on an ongoing basis – their livelihoods are always questioned and framed within a normatively white settler paradigm. Here O'Shane's story connects to Jett's narrative, whereby he marks Indigenous peoples as disruptive (e.g., they are considered angry) vis-à-vis their unwillingness to assimilate and accept the white-supremacist and settler colonial conditions plaguing their lives. Indeed, this kind of logic of understanding Indigenous peoples to be grateful for the conditions of white settler colonialism does an incredible injustice to the ongoing violence they experience – this violence is psychic, lived, and multidimensional (Greensmith, 2012; Million, 2013; O'Shane, 2015).

Moreover, Byrd's (2011) theorization of the function of Indigeneity as transit is important to consider in unpacking Jett's narrative. Here Byrd notes that transit is a "concept [that] suggests the multiple subjectivities and subjugations put into motion and made to move through notions of injury, grievance, and grievability as the United States deploys a paradigmatic Indianness to facilitate its imperial desires" (p. xxi). Byrd highlights how the necropolitics of eliminating Indigeneity forces the status of non-Indigenous peoples to exist indefinitely so that Indigenous peoples can be perpetually subjugated. Thus, there remains a relationship, even if it is skewed, to benefit white LGBTQ+ settlers like Jett. His narrative exposes how white supremacist and settler colonial logics construct people of colour as assimilateable and Indigenous peoples as too difficult to care for due to their anger since they are seemingly unwilling to assimilate – a tale early European settlers told themselves to justify Indigenous peoples' genocide (Talaga, 2017). Jett's narrative can be situated within the larger historical nexus in which the helping professions reside that regularly requires Indigenous peoples to stifle their anger – and indeed be content with their own genocide – and assimilate themselves into white settler normativity if they are ever to receive adequate support and care.

Upon completing our interview, Nicole, a 46-year-old, white, queer, cisgender woman who works as a program coordinator at a youth organization, shared an important story of how some Indigenous youth reacted to one of the voting workshops that happened at her queer organization. Her narrative highlights the ways queer organizations can normalize paternalistic care logics – whereby Indigenous youth, in this case, must participate in seemingly normal "Canadian" rituals of voting, separated from the ways the Canadian nation state contributes to ongoing violence of Indigenous communities and nations.

Q: Are there any additional issues you think need to be raised as part of this research?

A: Just thinking off the top of my head, one question might be: what are the needs of ... what are the needs expressed by the First Nations people that you have met? I can answer that. I find that the ones who self-identify and there are a range of personalities and peoples who are experiencing their own challenges for complex reasons so the voices come loaded. We have been challenged by Indigenous youth saying that the workshops we run do not speak to them. For example, we ran a workshop about how to vote. We wanted all of the youth to ask questions when voting. Yet, we received word that the workshop does not speak to First Nations youth. Before the last federal election we had a conversation about issues to consider before voting and one of the issues that came up was around First Nations solidarity. But because the staff were white, the youth challenged them saying, "you do not know what you are talking about, you are Othering me." The staff was saying, "well, we are actually trying to be allies and be in solidarity." So this workshop did not meet the youth's needs and they did not feel safe. I think it is about not wanting to have their issues outed in that environment. (03/13/13, Transcript 25, p. 7, Toronto, ON)

Nicole's narrative indicates that in the context of voting, once Indigenous youths' relationship to the Canadian nation state came up, the Indigenous youth attending the workshop argued that the helping professionals had no idea how these issues truly impacted Indigenous peoples. Nicole concluded by connecting the challenges Indigenous youth had with the voting workshop with that of not wanting their "issues" outed. However, what is missing from Nicole's narrative is her difficulty in considering how her leadership surrounding the voting workshop and investment in "the/our/my community" impacted how queer organizations operate. Constructing the Indigenous youth as "not feeling safe" and, as a result, viewing them as not wanting their issues "outed" can create the Indigenous youth voicing their concern or critique as "problems" who require specific care and attention. Nicole's narrative illustrated that Indigenous youth must vote and participate in a white settler colonial system that routinely marks Indigenous peoples as disposable. Indigenous peoples' disposability has been widely documented in the *National Inquiry into Missing and Murdered Indigenous Women and Girls*, discussed in the Introduction, particularly in white settlers ignoring the agency and expertise of Indigenous women, girls, and LGBTQ2S+ people. By dismissing the values and beliefs of Indigenous youth, reducing their frustration with her organization to simply not wanting their issues "outed," Nicole fails to understand the larger white settler colonial processes and practices in which queer organizations and helping professionals are entangled.

While Nicole's narrative highlights the relationship between the paternalism of queer organizations and the silencing of Indigenous youth's agency, similar to Jett, Justin's story addresses the ways Indigenous identity is erased from client-service user interactions. The white settler imaginary of counselling work – to focus on helping service users work through their immediate trauma – can often erase important and necessary conversations surrounding the conditions that make Indigenous identity impossible. Here, Justin, a 61-year-old, white, gay, cisgender man who works as a volunteer at a mental health organization, shared a story of working very closely with a psychiatrized, Indigenous, trans service user.

> Aboriginal people have been absent from any real conscious engagement in the agency and that was true for me too until I had a client whom I was very fond of. I worked with him off and on for a couple of years. This client had a very terrible traumatic history and also had a dissociative personality disorder. He was always suicidal and it was really difficult to do anything really effective with him. He recently died. Just before his death, a couple of months before he died, he disclosed that he was First Nations. He said, "oh I have just been part of a healing circle and I am going to do some sweat lodges and I have a spiritual mentor." I thought to myself, how did I miss that? How did I miss that? I was so focused on his growing up as a trans young person in far interland [sic] of Northern Ontario. Being First Nations is a really critical piece of his identity as well. (03/08/13, Transcript 21, p. 6, Toronto, ON)

Justin shared with me his deep discomfort about not asking this particular Indigenous, trans service user questions about their Indigenous identity. This experience of working with this particular Indigenous, trans service user provided an opportunity for Justin to reevaluate how Indigeneity was easily unimaginable and dismissible within the context of counselling within queer organizations. Justin's narrative provides a context to consider how the inability to imagine Indigenous peoples within queer organizations can result in the narrowing of practice approaches that can easily disconnect gender and sexuality from other axes of a service user's identity. As a result, Justin's narrative

points to possibilities for doing queer service delivery differently insofar as Indigeneity must be considered part of queer practice in order
to ensure that Indigenous people's identities and experiences are supported and affirmed. Justin's narrative also provides the context to
consider how white LGBTQ+ helping professionals cannot necessarily
tell if an Indigenous person is Indigenous. Thus, the culture of whiteness within queer organizations does not provide white LGBTQ+ helping professionals with the possibility that Indigenous peoples might
be Indigenous or that Indigenous peoples will present themselves in a
white-imagined stereotypical way or through racial descriptors of nonwhiteness that white people use to recognize difference and diversity.

Importantly, Justin articulated that this awakening – to do queer
service delivery differently – occurred through developing a positive
relationship with the Indigenous trans service user who was dying.
While we may read Justin's story as ultimately recognizing the need
to address a necessary gap within queer organizations, we also see
necropolitical care at work. In John's story, we see the ways the necropolitics of care shapes the seeming ability of helping professionals to
care for Indigenous, trans service users. Leslie speaks to the structural
realities of queer organizations – there are perceived to be policies in
place that in turn shape the practices of helping professionals. Leslie,
a 27-year-old mestiza trans woman who works and volunteers at a
large organization, discussed with me how trans Indigenous women
and trans women of colour are constructed as "problems" within her
respective organization and stated:

> I guess most of the trans women of colour and trans Aboriginal women
> that I know of are sex workers. They do not have a very good rela-
> tionship with my organization. Maybe they come in inebriated or high on
> something. However, I do not know the policies to deal with that. Usually
> they come in and there is no problem, they can get their food. For what-
> ever reason there might be an incident that prevents them from coming
> back. (01/04/13, Transcript 4, p. 4, Toronto, ON)

Leslie noted that, in her relationships with trans women of colour and
Indigenous trans women, they are typically accessing services at the
agency, as they are likely sex workers. Leslie posited that trans women
of colour and Indigenous trans women tend to have a contentious relationship with queer organizations since they are assumed routinely
to enter while they are on various substances. Yet, as Leslie articu-
lates, at her specific queer agency, there are no policies that suggest
that service users cannot come to the organization using substances.

Thus, alcoholism, as Thatcher argued, is often pinned onto the bodies of Indigenous (trans) people, and thus they are prohibited from utilizing the services at the organization – if they are caught. The seemingly ironic issue regarding substance use on the property of the queer organization is that the agency has a liquor licence, allowing respectable LGBTQ2S+ people, those who possess economic privilege, to attend events and purchase alcohol, even simultaneously with Alcohol Anonymous programming and the barring of Indigenous trans service users. The issue that remains is that only Indigenous peoples are removed from the queer organization generally and its programming for using substances, not all LGBTQ2S+ service users, highlighting the very real ways necropolitical care operates.

Skyler, a 25-year-old, mixed-race, genderqueer person who works at the same organization as Leslie as a part-time administrator, said: "The only time I do see First Nations [is] when they are coming in to use the washroom. Many of them are intoxicated and are asked to leave" (01/09/13, Transcript 7, p. 7, Toronto, ON). Leslie and Skyler's stories evoke stereotypes around how perceived or actual drunkenness or alcoholism is used to actively remove Indigenous peoples from queer organizations. Although Skyler indicated that the Indigenous peoples they see are intoxicated when entering their queer organization, Leslie notes that it is Indigenous (trans) peoples' perceived drunkenness that ensures that their relationship with the organization, and the services they so desperately need, remain fractured. Leslie and Skyler's narratives provide the context to consider how the perception of drunkenness and alcoholism is used to effectively remove Indigenous peoples from queer organizations, ultimately shaping their access to care and support.

While the stories of Leslie and Skyler contend that the white imaginary sees Indigenous peoples as "drunks," which is often used to bar them from queer organizations, Steve's story highlights the explicit removal of Indigenous peoples from queer spaces – they must receive "culturally appropriate" service elsewhere. As shared by the research participants in Chapter 2, queer organizations want to appear inclusive of difference and diversity, even when the particular services offered may not necessarily be suitable for, or culturally relevant to, Indigenous peoples. Steve, a 38-year-old, gay, Latino, cisgender man who works as a sexual-health coordinator at a large ASO, discussed with me how queer organizations try to make spaces more inclusive of 2-Spirited service users. As Steve indicated: "Let me be fair. At this organization, there are a lot of posters of 2-Spirits. [2-Spirited people] are [as] welcome as any other client. If they want something specifically for them, they are going to be referred [somewhere else]" (03/02/13, Transcript 20, p. 10, Toronto, ON). Steve's story illustrates how representations of 2-Spirited people alone may not necessarily translate into queer organizations' programming in culturally relevant or meaningful ways.

While Steve suggested that 2-Spirited people are as welcome "as any other client," he also said that, if they require additional or more-focused services, they will be sent somewhere else. Here, diversity is manufactured to depict the queer organization as inclusive, when in actuality Indigenous peoples are removed from the space entirely if they require "specialized services" – effectively creating the organization as a space that invites racial difference into its assumed whiteness. Steve's narrative does not exist in isolation; rather, it is a common practice among non-Indigenous LGBTQ+ helping professionals in Toronto, where Indigenous peoples are removed from mainstream, white-normed, queer organizations and referred out to Indigenous-led organizations, such as 2-Spirits. Consequently, due to the emergence of organizations like 2-Spirits, larger queer organizations, such as the one Steve worked at, can support LGBTQ2S+ people more generally and might therefore understand their work as disconnected from racism and settler colonialism.

While Steve's narrative highlights the seeming everyday and mundane practice of Indigenous exclusion through the necropolitics of care, Ryan's story proves how the everyday violence Indigenous peoples experience can be lost within the helping relationship. Ryan, a 34-year-old, white, gay, cisgender man with Indigenous ancestry who works as a sexual-health counsellor at a sexual-health organization, discussed with me the everyday impacts of colonialism on Indigenous women and spoke about an HIV/AIDS testing satellite at a local queer organization.

> When we were testing at the [organization name removed], we did not anticipate it, but we saw a lot of trans women who self-identified as Aboriginal and who were also involved in sex work. These women were very proud of their culture and very aware, but they are living these miserable grimy lives. Everyone likes to talk about the theoretical legacy of colonialism, but when you actually see people on their traditional land and it is rightly theirs, and they are slamming meth in the bathroom of McDonalds, where is the analysis then? (03/09/13, Transcript 23, p. 3, Toronto, ON)

Ryan's statement highlights that the analysis of the effects of colonialism on Indigenous people's lives is "theoretical," and therefore dismissible. Ryan's narrative illustrates how such a focus on substance use alone, for helping professionals, is enough of a "reality" to prevent or toss out any "theoretical" critique of the (settler) colonialism within Indigenous people's lives. Reducing Indigenous trans women to pathological or "problems," specifically constructing them as living "miserable grimy lives," produces them to be outside of neoliberal models of care, and, consequently, to be unworthy of care.

In essence, Ryan's narrative reproduces all-too-familiar necropolitical constructions of Indigenous peoples that make their lives and encounters with trauma dismissible and disposable. Narratives that helping professionals use to depict Indigenous peoples as abject, in particular their experiences of poverty or drug use, provides an avenue for queer helping professionals, like Ryan, who ironically has Indigenous ancestry, to disconnect a critique of settler colonialism from the practices used within queer organizations. Within Ryan's narrative, he implies that it is only the Indigenous peoples who can evict themselves from their pathological or "problem" status and become worthy of adequate support or care – further supporting and normalizing the conditions of white settler colonialism and necropolitical care deeply embedded within queer organizations and the helping ethos of non-Indigenous LGBTQ+ helping professionals.

While Ryan's narrative highlights the sheer disposability of Indigenous peoples and a "theoretical" understanding of colonialism that plagues their lives, Amanda affirms that, within the context of substance-use treatment, Indigenous peoples must receive different supports than non-Indigenous LGBTQ+ service users. Lisa contends that the necropolitical construction of Indigenous peoples transcends Canada and has become a transnational phenomenon – tropes that travel to places like Jamaica. Lisa, a 46-year-old, mixed-race, cisgender lesbian who works as a newcomer-service coordinator at a large queer organization, discussed with me how her perception of Indigenous peoples changed after moving to Canada.

> My portrayal of First Nations persons was through the very few that I ever met who were drunk, who were living on the reserves, and gambled a lot. This perception of First Nations persons is similar to how my own people are viewed. It is not the best depiction of First Nations persons but it is all that I have been exposed to. I never heard of Aboriginal people until I landed here. (01/15/13, Transcript 9, p. 1, Toronto, ON)

Lisa's narrative exposes the discourses used depicting Indigenous peoples as "deficits," a similar trope used to stereotype Jamaicans. Lisa drew from her own experiences as a mixed-race woman to suggest potential cross-racial/transnational understandings of the racial and (settler) colonial stereotyping of Indigenous peoples. Lisa acknowledged that there are white-supremacist and settler colonial narratives of both Indigenous peoples and Black peoples in the Americas, which she was compelled to take on when she arrived in Canada and worked with "newcomers." Thus, Lisa's narrative provides an opportunity to consider how white settler colonialism marginalizes and subjugates Indigenous peoples and Black people within and outside of queer organizations.

The stories shared by some of the research participants highlight the seemingly quotidian narratives of Indigenous peoples as "deficits," "problems," and/or "pathological" within the context of queer organizations. The normalcy of these stories must be questioned so as to disrupt the ways white settler colonialism enters into the ways queer organizations function – including the ways non-Indigenous LGBTQ+ helping professionals work with and imagine Indigenous peoples. Importantly, these stories highlight that, despite queer organizations' ability to claim that they are diverse and welcoming of diversity, they in fact contribute to the reproduction and normalization of necropolitical care within queer organizations. The stories of Indigeneity here are immersed in narratives of white settler goodness whereby the very stories of violence, exclusion, and neglect are used to uplift the helping professionals themselves and consequently the organizations they work within.

The Necropolitics of Practice

By engaging with the narratives offered by non-Indigenous LGBTQ+ helping professionals, it is clear that Indigenous peoples are routinely positioned – through the practice of necropolitics – as unimaginable, unworthy of care, or too difficult to care for. Indeed, the necropolitical constructions of Indigenous peoples as "problems" and as "pathological" easily allow for most white LGBTQ+ helping professionals to distance themselves and their work from how white settler colonialism remains firmly intact and operationalized within queer organizations. Consequently, many of the research participants I encountered were perfectly content with articulating that Indigenous difference is intact, which furthered their ability to at once care for Indigeneity – as a means to an end – while also evicting Indigenous peoples from queer spaces of belonging or worth. As I highlighted in Chapter 2, the research participant's investment in Indigenous inclusion is connected to tropes of nation-building – multicultural diversity – that is, they were working towards an ideological model of inclusion.

Despite the overwhelming normalcy of white settler colonialism within the walls of queer organizations and the practice approaches of helping professionals, some research participants, such as Justin and Lisa, provided possibilities for working against the "deficit" narratives associated with Indigenous inclusion and Indigenous peoples. Popular stereotypes of drunkenness that are pinned onto Indigenous peoples are sustained as they are asked to leave the premises, in the case of Lisa and Skyler's stories, further maintaining the normativity of whiteness and settler colonialism within queer organizations whereby white LGBTQ+ peoples are produced as the most worthy of care. Here, white settler colonialism is sustained by actively removing Indigenous peoples from queer spaces of belonging or worth. As a result, the day-to-day work of white LGBTQ+ helping professionals produces Indigeneity as an additive to the foundation of the organization's mandate around gender and sexuality. The nature of identity within queer organizations – "add and stir" or cultural competency methods/models – further perpetuates the individuality of Indigenous people's concerns and their experiences of white supremacy and settler colonialism. I have illustrated how queer organizations have difficulty understanding Indigenous peoples in their motivations and also their caring frameworks. Despite this, some research participants' narratives, in particular Justin and Lisa's, provide an opportunity for Indigenous peoples and settler colonialism to be taken seriously – as an urgent and necessary condition of queer organizations and the work done by non-Indigenous LGBTQ+ helping professionals.

It is clear from the narratives offered earlier by the research participants that there is a critical urgency to meaningfully include a white settler colonial analytic within queer organizations and practice. This erasure, one that foregrounds queer organizations within the white settler colonial logics and institutions, furthers the neoliberal and necropolitical perceptions that Indigenous peoples are to alleviate their harm. Yet, these logics used to further sustain white settler colonialism within queer organizations produce a separatist logic whereby Indigenous peoples become unimaginable from the politics of care practised by non-Indigenous LGBTQ+ helping professionals. Consequently, this politics of care, one that uplifts the needs, desires, and bodies of white LGBTQ+ peoples, further sustains a culture of white settler colonialism so embedded within contemporary life in Canada. As a result, the research participants' narratives provide an opportunity to reconsider queer organizations as a site for emancipation, asking "who is positioned as worthy of care?"

If Indigenous peoples are imagined to be outside of queer organizations, it is a dire and necessary intervention to address how queer organizations, as white settler colonial institutions, further sustain and contribute to genocide. As a result, one important intervention, as some of the research participants' narratives highlight, is to incorporate a white settler colonial analytic within the context of queer organizations so that Indigenous peoples' ongoing and multigenerational hauntings of white settler colonialism are addressed. A white settler colonial analytic would provide an opportunity for non-Indigenous LGBTQ+ helping professionals to take the needs and experiences of Indigenous peoples seriously, while simultaneously putting a stop to a separatist framework that further places the responsibility to create Indigenous-led service organizations onto the backs of Indigenous organizations. Indeed, while the non-Indigenous LGBTQ+ helping professionals interviewed continually utilize their imaginings of queerness to exclude Indigenous peoples, the work they do within the white walls of the queer organization operates within the context of complicity. Indeed, situating the work done within queer organizations within the lexicon of white, queer complicity foregrounds the action taken within a larger settler colonial framework. The language of complicity also highlights the need for non-Indigenous LGBTQ+ helping professionals and queer organizations alike to work towards eliminating all sorts of violence enacted on the bodies of BIPOC.

Chapter Five

A Call to Action: Queerness, Complicity, and Deflecting Responsibility

A decolonial queer praxis requires that we engage in the complexities of re-orienting ourselves away from White supremacist logics and systems and toward more respectful and accountable ways of being in relation to one another and the lands we live on, while not appropriating Indigenous knowledge. (Hunt & Holmes, 2015, p. 168)

Introduction

In her ground-breaking book *Being Good, Being White: White Complicity, White Moral Responsibility, and Social Justice Pedagogy*, Barbara Applebaum (2011) theorized the various ways in which the systemically advantaged (white subjects) are complicit in structural injustice (white supremacy). For Applebaum, "'the white complicity claim' maintains that white people, through the practices of whiteness and by benefiting from white privilege, contribute to the maintenance of systemic racial injustice" (p. 3). In theorizing white complicity, Applebaum notes that simply acknowledging one's involvement in and relationship to systemic injustice is not enough to challenge how white supremacy structures everyday life – white people must work towards dismantling the very systems from which they benefit. Naming white complicity provides white people the opportunity to locate their whiteness structurally and invites whites themselves to make change to combat racism (Applebaum, 2011; DiAngelo, 2018; Hill-Collins, 2003).

While Applebaum's work on white complicity shifts discussions away from individual articulations of privilege, her work does not explicitly address the ways theories of white complicity may sustain and normalize historical and contemporary forms of settler colonialism. To ignore or disconnect settler colonial formations from white supremacy can often do a disservice to the interlocking nature of violence Indigenous peoples continue to face. Settler colonialism naturalizes the erasure, assimilation, and dispossession of Indigenous peoples, communities, nations, and lands. As such, a settler colonial analytic provides the capacity to address "the logic[s] of superiority, of primacy, [and] of genocide" (Mikdashi, 2013, p. 32). As Susanne Waldorf (2012) argues in her critique of Applebaum's work, "complicity in settler colonialism is also a matter of existing or being on land that was and continues to be stolen from Indigenous peoples" (p. 39). While theories of white complicity have provided necessary criticisms of structural racism in the lives of white people and their seemingly "good" actions and intentions, as a theory it must engage with the interlocking impact of settler colonialism so as not to erase the historical and contemporary violence Indigenous peoples continue to face.

Complicity, then, draws attention to the need for a call to action – to acknowledge and work against systems of oppression from which dominant subjects benefit. Cannon (2012) notes that white settlers and people of colour have a *responsibility* to address the uneven and life-altering impacts of white settler colonialism facing Indigenous peoples, communities, and nations. Cannon is not alone in calling attention to the complicities of non-Indigenous peoples: they must take responsibility for historical and contemporary wrongdoings of settler colonialism (Alfred, 2005, 2009; Cannon, 2012; Dion, 2009; Monture-Angus, 1995, 1999; Talaga, 2017; Vowel, 2018). Notably, this call to action on the part of non-Indigenous peoples has been sparked by Eve Tuck and K. Wayne Yang's (2012) important essay *Decolonization is not a Metaphor*, where they critique the use of decolonization within social-justice endeavours and movements, arguing that: "when metaphor invades decolonization, it kills the very possibility of decolonization; it recentres whiteness, it resettles theory, it extends innocence to the settler, it entertains a settler future" (p. 3). As a metaphor, decolonization has the potential to lose its connection to materiality and the land and to continue white settler colonial projects.

Queer organizations are sites that often mobilize the language of decolonization and Indigenous solidarity – yet their in/action often goes unexamined. This chapter engages the ways non-Indigenous LGBTQ+ helping professionals may be complicit in ongoing white settler colonial projects. As noted in Chapter 2, queer organizations become important sites to examine the materiality of non-Indigenous LGBTQ+ helping professionals' complicity, as engagements with Indigenous peoples often are sedimented within discourses of inclusion, diversity, and difference. Queer organizations, with their investments in all things LGBTQ2S+, are primarily dedicated to addressing inequalities that manifest through cisheterosexism. And these organizations are not being challenged for their ability to do such important work in that area; rather, what is at stake here is how queer organizations and non-Indigenous LGBTQ+ helping professionals alike often use Indigenous peoples in their claims of being woke, antioppressive, or doing queer work.

In order to address the various and complex ways non-Indigenous LGBTQ+ peoples may be complicit in the erasure, dispossession, and genocide of Indigenous peoples specifically, this chapter asks: how do the stories of non-Indigenous LGBTQ+ helping professionals shape how they come to know, think about, and understand their own roles and responsibilities in addressing the complexities of white supremacy and settler colonialism? This chapter focuses heavily on the experiences of white people as always connected to the interlocking violence of white supremacy and settler colonialism. My use of *non-Indigenous* is more pointed; that is, the term is used to hail white settlers, Black people, and people of colour in their potential complicities in sustaining white settler colonial violence. However, in discussing the imbrication of enslavement and white settler colonialism, Tiffany Lethabo King (2015) notes that "white settlers and Black people are not ontological/structural equivalents in this hemisphere" (p. 67). Given the surge of critical writing in Black Studies and Indigenous Studies on Black peoples' relationship to white settler colonialism, I engage "non-Indigenous" in understanding the complexities and possibilities therein.

Many critical Indigenous studies scholars have called out the ways global systems of inequality routinely marginalize Indigenous peoples (Amadahy & Lawrence, 2009; Byrd, 2011; Cannon, 2012; Fujikane & Okamura, 2008; Jafri, 2012, 2013; King, 2015; Lawrence & Dua, 2005; Vowel, 2018). Thus, in order to address the ways white supremacy and settler colonialism are connected to and produced within queer organizations in Toronto, I first theorize the ways in which innocence and complicity continue to shape white LGBTQ+ people and their understandings of responsibility. Next, I situate the larger theorization of complicity within the narratives offered by the non-Indigenous research participants. Finally, I offer a set of conclusions as a mode to consider the ways non-Indigenous LGBTQ+ helping professionals might address their complicities in white settler colonialism in the form of action: decolonization. The resulting discussion provides an avenue to consider how non-Indigenous LGBTQ+ peoples might work within and outside the neoliberal confines of queer organizations and social movements in Toronto and beyond and address their responsibilities in undoing white settler colonial projects.

Theorizing Innocence and Complicity

In order to conceptualize how non-Indigenous LGBTQ+ helping professionals move towards assertions of innocence, and indeed their own complicities in white settler colonialism and its projects, it is important to look at how *innocence* is defined and has been theorized. *Innocence* refers to "the belief that because we are ourselves in a subordinate position, we are unimplicated in the oppression of others" (Fellows & Razack, 1998, p. 339). As Patricia Hill-Collins (2003) notes, "we typically fail to see how our thoughts and actions uphold someone else's subordination" (p. 25). This failure to recognize how claims of being "only-marginalized" subjects, or only experiencing trauma, can signify complicity in others' oppression, which illustrates that participation in the marginalization of others requires ongoing interrogation on the part of privileged subjects. Mary Louise Fellows and Sherene Razack outlined how, in deflecting their attachments to and investments in white supremacy, white women often naturalize a hierarchical model of oppression, whereby their experiences of sexism are deemed most concerning and valuable – a perspective worth criticizing as white women's whiteness is omitted when making such a claim.

In centralizing their experiences of sexism, white women "race to innocence" by disconnecting from how they may very well contribute to "the oppression of others" by deflecting their responsibility in white supremacist projects (Fellows & Razack, 1998, p. 340). The unmarked nature of whiteness allows for white subjects (e.g., white poor people, white LGBTQ+ people) to understand their actions as neutral and thus see themselves as unimplicated in systems of white supremacy, settler colonialism, and projects of nation-building (Schick & McNinch, 2009). The work here on white innocence provides the theoretical backdrop to expose and address how white LGBTQ+ helping professionals – who are overrepresented within queer organizations in downtown Toronto (see research participant demographics in **Table 1**) – continue to participate in and sustain white supremacy.

Yet, an analysis of whiteness alone does not adequately address the interlocking nature of whiteness and settler colonialism. In discussing this connection, Razack (2002) argued that investments of white settler innocence, which allow for whites and their descendants easily to understand themselves as naturally connected to the land, further erase the presence of Indigenous peoples. Evocations of white settler innocence impede on the ability of whites to consider the everyday conditions contributing to the white settler colonial projects they often belong to. Celia Haig-Brown (2009) also alluded to notions of settler innocence when asking her non-Indigenous preservice teachers to consider how the land they reside on – as a place they have made or might be able to call home – is contested. Moreover, as Cannon (2012) argued, for Indigenous decolonization to prevail, BIPOC and whites alike must be conscious of the land they reside on, the histories of colonial violence that created the conditions connected to the land, and of the already-formed relationships they have with Indigenous peoples.

Giwa and I (2013) have noted that the question of who or who is not a settler is unproductive; the analytic rests within the terrain of identity politics and the individual claiming the settler identity. Instead, Tuck and Yang (2012) suggest that all non-Indigenous peoples (regardless of their history or relationships to settler colonialism) are contributors to the violence of white settler colonialism and contended that they must move beyond evocations of settler innocence, described as "excuses, distractions, and diversions from decolonization" (p. 10). While Tuck and Yang (2012) implicate all non-Indigenous peoples as a consciousness-raising tactic, they do so without fully engaging with the global networks of white supremacy and colonialism Black people and people of colour live within and through (Amadahy & Lawrence, 2009; Byrd, 2011; Cannon, 2012; Fujikane & Okamura, 2008; Jafri, 2012, 2013; King, 2015; Lawrence & Dua, 2005; Vowel, 2018). Shaista Patel et al. (2015) note: "Complicity cannot be theorised in isolation. Complicity in one structure does not erase complicities in others. Rather, they are always enabled by, and enable other structures of complicity" (p. 13). Black people and people of colour may be complicit in white settler colonialism; however, their complicity must be understood and engaged differently – through the context of transatlantic enslavement, migration and forced exile, and/or transnational labour patterns (Thobani, 2007). After all, Black people and people of colour do not accrue the benefits of white supremacy in the same way as white settlers and their descendants.

The resulting discussion of settler innocence and complicity within this chapter considers the fissures in history that separate white people from Black people and people of colour by highlighting the important differences within their relationships to white settler colonialism. This chapter shows the processes and practices of queer organizations, where non-Indigenous LGBTQ+ helping professionals move towards settler innocence somewhat differently – as minoritized LGBTQ+ subjects. I extend Tuck and Yang's (2012) analysis on innocence to bring discussions of whiteness, queerness, and settler colonialism into the conversation. I illustrate that, in order to address the workings of white settler colonialism within the context of queer organizations in Toronto, one must consider how white LGBTQ+ people's evocations of innocence are connected to their own (or their organization's) understandings and articulations of (white) LGBTQ+ politics in Canada, as noted in Chapter 2.

As discussed in Chapter 1, the inception of queer organizations, as a modern (white settler colonial) project, occurred in conjunction with the civil rights movement, deeply tying queer politics and communities to progress. As Scott Morgensen (2011b) argued, "queers within a white settler state ... become modern through homonationalist participation in colonial and imperial rule that awards citizenship for defending the state and educating subject peoples in civilizational values, including sexual modernity" (p. 226). White LGBTQ+ peoples are required to justify their work within their pretence of a global LGBTQ2S+ "community" as well as appeal to white settler multiculturalism by folding BIPOC into projects that still reproduce white settler colonial power relations and structures of violence. While many Indigenous scholars have noted the complexities that arise in naming one's complicities in white settler colonialism, it is equally important to situate critiques of queer complicity within the lexicon of whiteness. We cannot erase the multifaceted ways whiteness *and* settler colonialism work together to marginalize and inflict violence upon BIPOC.

To expose the potential complicities of non-Indigenous LGBTQ+ people in white settler colonialism, I home in on the ways queerness is typically conflated with and connected to whiteness (Muñoz, 1999). This queerness is (re)produced within queer organizations and thus worthy of exploration. James McNinch (2008) homed in on the very real effects of homophobic violence and trauma that gay, cisgender men experience in rural Saskatchewan and described that the everyday experience of marginalization "connects '(us) fags' and '(them) Indian[s],' as well as any group with markings of difference" (p. 90). McNinch draws attention towards the potential connections between queers and Indigenous peoples as a helpful starting point; however, in doing so, McNinch's work can easily erase their differences and experiences with systemic oppression and institutional violence. In particular, McNinch's analogy creates LGBTQ2S+ BIPOC as subjects who cannot bridge the single imaginary of (white) queerness and (straight) Others. Within this particular reading, perhaps there seems to be a missed opportunity surrounding how interlocking theories of race, nation, and homophobia might work together to create alliances that may not have ever before been imagined or formulated between "'us (fags)' and '(them) Indians'" (p. 90).

As bell hooks (1988) reminds us, our differences may indeed allow for solidarity among groups who can develop relationships precisely because they understand how they may contribute to the problem – rather than the solution. This recognition of difference would do away with simplistic, flat (straight?) articulations of inequality that conflate histories of colonization with that of cisheterosexism and allow for "us (fags)" to think differently about how non-Indigenous LGBTQ+ peoples may work with Indigenous peoples respectfully and responsibly. While McNinch (2008) seems to conflate the oppressive (white) queers and (straight) Indigenous peoples, Margot Francis's (2011) work discussed how whiteness is mobilized within the queer subversions and performative politics of Shawna Dempsey and Lorri Millan's "Lesbian National Parks and Services" (LNPS). The LNPS performance intends to destabilize the heteromasculinity attached to wilderness spaces, like national parks, and queer these spaces through the performers' articulations and understandings of being lesbians (Francis, 2011). As Francis argued, within these queer subversions, the LNPS performance artists rely "on taken-for-granted ideas about the innocent character of the landscape they inhabit to serve as the backdrop for a performative challenge to masculinist and heteronormative assumptions" (p. 113). Within these disruptions of white cisheteromasculinity, the LNPS performers do not outwardly address the contradictions that exist within their processes and practices of white settler colonialism. As Francis suggested, the LNPS performers' move towards white innocence is a way to remain unimplicated in projects of white supremacy. However, this can also erase the possibility of white lesbians upholding and maintaining settler colonialism as they critique the whiteness of cisheteromasculinity. In terms of queer complicity, then, the works of Francis and McNinch (2008) provide important theoretical avenues to address how (white) queers, in divergent ways, might easily deflect their relationship to white settler colonialism.

(White) Queer Complicities

While theories of innocence and complicity articulate privileged subjects' investments in domination, the relationship between non-Indigenous LGBTQ+ helping professionals and white settler colonialism has not been fully examined. Evolving out of the narratives of the research participants, three major themes emerged: (1) moving to innocence, (2) complicity as inclusion, and (3) deflections of responsibility.

These findings reflect the ways in which the research participants articulated their own understandings of queer organizations and the extent
to which Indigenous peoples and nations might be better included.
I consider how some white LGBTQ+ helping professionals continue to
claim innocence in terms of the ongoing oppression of BIPOC.

Moving to Innocence

The following narratives depict how some white LGBTQ+ helping professionals imagine helping work within queer organizations through
the lens of trauma – as very real experiences of cisheterosexism must
be addressed among service users. The narratives of trauma that are
evoked within queer organizations operate to sustain the perception
that non-Indigenous LGBTQ+ peoples can only experience oppression due to their sexual and/or gendered minority status. In theorizing trauma, I utilize the important work of Brown (1995), Linklater
(2014), and Million (2013). Brown describes trauma as a "wounded
attachment," whereby subjects connect their experiences of violence
to identity-based political movements and, in doing so, recentre their
pain. I note that being "in pain" can often preclude subjects from acting responsibly to the pressing needs of BIPOC. Linklater (2014) notes
that, while the concept of trauma may indeed come from the Western
canon, it has utility in understanding Indigenous peoples' "responses
to ... injury" (p. 22) including but not limited to the effects of settler
colonialism.

Million (2013) contends that the acknowledgment of Indigenous
peoples' trauma has turned into industry within helping professions
globally, whereby Indigenous peoples are only ever imagined as "dam-
aged" and in need of saving. This chapter pays particular attention to
how non-Indigenous LGBTQ+ peoples' trauma (or our queer wounds)
gets used as the basis for doing particular kinds of queer helping work
and can inadvertently produce non-Indigenous LGBTQ+ helping professionals as complicit. The interviewees' stories of trauma articulate a
sense of urgency and necessity to do the work within queer organizations in Toronto – and how this queer pain shapes their imaginations
of service users, their motivations for doing queer work, and indeed
how queer organizations, communities, and politics in Canada are
imagined.

Josh, a 53-year-old, South Asian, queer, cisgender man who works as
a public educator at an Ontario-wide organization, discussed how such
a focus on experiences of "gay" trauma can sometimes be unproductive

and disconnected from his own experiences as a queer person of colour. As Josh explained:

> [At] conferences I see gay men whining about what Catholicism and Christianity has done. I am like "oh for heaven[s] sake you are 50 years old get over it, get a grip. Stop blaming your mom and dad and the Church for everything that has happened to you." I look at the way Western gay culture has been perpetuated and it does not in any way enlighten me. I try to consciously distance myself from it. (02/25/13, Transcript 17, p. 12, Toronto, ON)

Josh's narrative comes out of a larger discussion of the whiteness of gayness and the representations of respectability within LGBTQ2S+ communities in Toronto. Josh discussed how his experiences as a queer person of colour do not necessarily fit within "Western gay culture." In the context of the community-based and academic conferences Josh goes to, white, gay, cisgender men typically evoke the common perception that one's religious upbringing is antigay, and thus they continue to experience trauma and pain in their present out of those painful (religious) experiences. Josh noted that this perception of trauma, popularized by white, gay, cisgender men, is not representative of his own experiences as a queer person of colour. Josh argued that the imminent focus on the trauma experienced by a white, gay, cisgender man with a Christian or Catholic upbringing is unhelpful, since it focuses on blame, recentres the whiteness of gayness, and erases gay cisgender men raised in, for example, Hindu, Buddhist, Muslim, and Jewish families. Echoing Linklater (2014) and Million (2013), homing in on the violence of (religious) trauma as a "singular"' form of oppression creates a hierarchy within evocations of trauma through which Indigenous peoples' contemporary experiences of genocide and conquest become disconnected.

In response to the routine, repetitive trauma gay men experience, Ryan, a 34-year-old, white, gay, cisgender man with Indigenous ancestry who works as a sexual-health counsellor at a sexual-health organization, said: "I just feel that gay men are remarkably well suited to dealing with shit hands. In so many areas of our lives, everything is shit and it is accepted and it is fine … it mystifies me that it is acceptable" (03/09/13, Transcript 23, p. 6, Toronto, ON). Ryan outlined the repetitive trauma that gay cisgender men experience within their daily lives. Ryan's narrative is problematic because it invokes a universalizing idea of gayness as experiencing only oppression, which can uplift the pain of white, gay, cisgender men and leaves their claim to being wounded unavailable to critiques of how their pain is experienced through their whiteness. Ryan's understanding of "shit hands" experienced through gay oppression in particular excludes the multifaceted ways in which violent systems of oppression impact others marginalized by cishetero-sexism who may not necessarily be, or not want to identify as, "gay." That is, the version of "shit hands" evoked by Ryan through his lexicon erases the ways BIPOC, who are routinely produced as straight, are erased from experiencing trauma or pain.

Additionally, Brandon, a 53-year-old, gay, white, cisgender man who works as a community-based researcher at a large ASO, discussed with me his thoughts on how there are similarities between the trauma experienced by HIV-positive gay cisgender men and that of Indigenous peoples.

> Q: What is some of the learning that you are getting out of working within your organization?
> A: That we have things to learn from the Aboriginal community so a lot of the tools that we are developing ... even the holistic model ... honour-ing that we are working on Native lands ... I came across the trauma informed tool kit, which actually came out of [a province in Canada] with a larger Aboriginal influence on its development. It talked about historical trauma. They did not just grow up invalidated for what they did but for who I was. That actually really resonated with me as a gay man [and] informs the work that I do in terms of expanding my own awareness around what does it mean to be Othered. (03/09/13, Tran-script 22, p. 6, Toronto, ON)

Brandon's narrative discusses how his learning shifted around the work that he does through a perceived connection to Indigenous peoples and their experiences of (colonial?) trauma. This connection Brandon sees occurs through considering experiences of invalidation as shared. Yet, within Brandon's narrative, he makes a switch from "they" to "I," since the category "gay" cannot be shared and is thus claimed for himself – no matter who (Indigenous or non-Indigenous) is inhabiting it. During Brandon's discussion, he at first noted that Indigenous differences must be acknowledged. Yet, within the particular slippage from "they" to "I," Brandon used (white) gay identity as a way to dissolve difference when considering the trauma or pain shared by gay, cisgender men and Indigenous peoples' experience. Here, gayness becomes produced as universal – a cross-cultural phenomenon that grants white, gay, cisgender men "access" to the experiences of (straight) Indigenous peoples whom they otherwise would not be able to say they understand.

Returning to McNinch's work, Brandon's narrative shows an attempt to bridge a gap between (white) gay, cisgender men and (straight) Indigenous peoples, particularly where he erases the differing experiences of invalidation, trauma, and being Othered. As Linklater (2014) and Million (2013) have argued, Indigenous peoples' trauma results from their multigenerational experiences of white settler colonial violence that is still occurring in the present day. Thus, the residual (heteronormative) trauma experienced by (white) gay, cisgender men cannot be equalized to that of (straight) Indigenous peoples' experiences of colonial violence. Brandon's narrative provides the context to consider how Indigenous peoples' traumatic experiences of white settler colonialism become folded into a universalizing trauma that is then consumed by white, gay, cisgender men.

In connection to Brandon's narrative on the similarities of trauma between white, gay, cisgender men and Indigenous peoples, Brett, a 31-year-old, white, queer, genderqueer person who works as a part-time relief worker at a sexual health organization, discussed why it is important to consider the impact of colonialism and decolonization within the work that they do.

> We need to acknowledge that we live on colonized lands and that we have some major cultural violence going on around Aboriginal people. But then also between the links between the idea of colonialism, decolonization and how that might be applied to other aspects of our [queer] lives and identities. How are queer people colonized by straight people? (04/30/13, Transcript 38, p. 2–3, Toronto, ON)

Brett's narrative addresses how colonialism continues to inflict violence upon Indigenous peoples and the need for decolonization to occur. In discussing the connection decolonization has to other axes of oppression, Brett asked: "how are queer people colonized by straight people?" By asking this question, Brett can potentially erase the historical and contemporary differences in power between white queers and Indigenous peoples within the white settler society we live in – specifically, how white settler colonialism invites white queer settlers to participate in its violent projects of Indigenous elimination and dispossession. More importantly, Brett's turn of phrase illustrates how (white) queerness is conflated with Indigenous peoples' experiences of trauma and used as the basis from which to interpret any form of trauma, with the result being that, if Indigenous peoples are colonized, then that must mean that queers are colonized too.

Although queer organizations are flourishing and developing rigorous LGBTQ2S+ programming and supports for their service users, it is clear from some of the white research participants' narratives that whiteness remains normalized and the differences between white queers and Indigenous peoples are made to dissolve when experiences of queer (gay?) trauma are centred. A hyperfocus surrounding trauma and its alleviation can constrain queer organizations and the ability of their workers to effectively decolonize – especially when they consider themselves as experiencing only oppression. While the trauma experienced by white LGBTQ+ helping professionals comes to constrain the delivery of queer services and the imagination of who is or can be queer, it is also essential to consider how Indigeneity is imagined within queer organizations. Indigenous peoples and cultures continue to be included, often as a symbolic gesture, by white LGBTQ+ helping professionals, which ultimately fuels white settler colonial logics through deflections of responsibility within and outside of queer organizations.

Complicity as Inclusion

The narratives around Indigenous peoples' inclusion are important to consider insofar as they can easily reinscribe normatively white expressions of queer organizations. Many of the research participants discussed how Indigenous peoples could be included within the context of queer organizations. In talking about what queer organizations could do differently to be more inclusive of Indigenous peoples, John, a 54-year-old, white, gay, cisgender man who has worked in various positions and organizations, illustrated that there are appropriate avenues for helping professionals to follow.

Q: What shape would your programs you are involved in take if they were designed to address the needs of Aboriginal people?

A: It would be developed by Aboriginal people for Aboriginal people. Whatever advisory groups or whatever would be [developed would] largely consist of Aboriginal people. I imagine there would be all sorts of community consultations and needs assessments that would specifically ask Aboriginal people what kinds of services they need ... and the hiring of counseling staff or whatever would be from that community and the services would ... reflec[t] what the needs assessment would be for them and would be evaluated on an ongoing basis with service users and community people and ongoing connections would happen with other Aboriginal organizations to get ongoing feedback around its effectiveness. (03/21/13, Transcript 30, p. 12, Toronto, ON)

It is important to locate the research participants' narratives within a larger historical critique of the helping professions, which illustrates that it is composed of institutions founded upon the death and disappearance of Indigenous peoples. White settler helping professionals have been told for years that organizations need to stop barring Indigenous participation, permit Indigenous helping professionals access to Indigenous service users, redirect Indigenous service users to Indigenous organizations, and grant forms of control over Indigenous organizations to Indigenous peoples and communities. John's narrative indicates that white LGBTQ+ helping professionals must consult with and, indeed, let Indigenous peoples and communities have primary say about how queer organizations should operate. However, this queer organizational model is saturated in neoliberal logics insofar as the appropriateness of the helping work is not based on Indigenous communities' wants and needs; rather, the helping work is deemed appropriate only if a needs assessment is measured and deemed effective. This version of *inclusive* queer organizations illustrates how the effectiveness of programs outweighs the accountability of white LGBTQ+ helping professionals (and queer organizations in Toronto) to Indigenous peoples and communities. Moreover, it erases the already well-established work of Indigenous organizations in Toronto (e.g., 2-Spirits and the Native Youth Sexual Health Network[1]).

Another example of how Indigenous peoples' perspectives can be included within queer organizations came from Cassandra, a 29-year-old, white, lesbian, cisgender woman who works as an addictions counsellor at a large mental health organization:

Q: How do Aboriginal peoples fit into your motivations in doing this work?
A: I think there are probably ways in which we could incorporate teaching and form a culturally competent space. Not to have myself deliver that, but to have some of our colleagues in the Aboriginal services deliver. (02/28/13, Transcript 18, p. 9, Toronto, ON)

Cassandra's narrative illustrates that a queer-services delivery model for Indigenous peoples would need to be more culturally competent than it already is in her organization. However, the inclusion of cultural competency, in Cassandra's estimation, should not come from her but instead her Indigenous colleagues. Cassandra's narrative points to how the inclusion of Indigeneity within queer organizations must be framed within a culturally competent approach, which can be criticized as reproducing cultural and racial stereotypes (DiAngelo, 2018; Linklater, 2014; Pon, 2009; St. Denis, 2011). Cassandra's approach to thinking about queer organizations differently includes placing Indigeneity, Indigenous culture, and teachings within a queer organizational structure that might not necessarily ever meet the needs of Indigenous peoples or communities, and Cassandra does not welcome this model of inclusion or competency, as the work is to be done solely by Indigenous peoples themselves. Utilizing a culturally competent approach within queer organizations when working with Indigenous peoples can lead non-Indigenous LGBTQ+ helping professionals to think in terms of cultural inclusion alone – a framework and practice approach made possible through colonial modernity. This move displaces urgent and necessary attention away from its structure, while simultaneously requiring Indigenous peoples to "do the work," further placing the responsibility of culture and inclusion onto them.

Josh, a 53-year-old, South Asian, queer, cisgender man who works as a public educator at an Ontario-wide organization, spoke with me about how evoking the responsibility of white people, specifically in the form of land recognition, can result in meaningless gestures of inclusion. As he shared:

> We do the usual tokenistic sort of declaring that we are on stolen land and that we have never recognized treaties and all that kind of stuff. It is not that we are giving back the land anytime soon. [Laughs]. So we do that disclosure but I think it is okay but I really wonder what it means to somebody who is First Nations sitting there. Does it make them feel any better [about] the historical persecution? ... I think we have a long way to go but also I am not the one to make these decisions. People often say to me: "well you are racialized because you think it is an issue." The white people [need to start] saying we need to take the steps to show that we actually genuinely care or want to make the change. (02/25/13, Transcript 17, p. 10, Toronto, ON)

Josh's powerful narrative illustrates how declarations of the land as stolen – in this case, referring to Toronto as the Mississaugas of the New Credit First Nation – during queer conferences and/or workshops makes him feel uneasy. Josh asked if such declarations adequately address the ongoing (historical) prosecution of Indigenous peoples. Within Josh's queer-of-colour criticism of land recognition, he contended that it should no longer be the sole responsibility of people of colour to address white supremacy and settler colonialism as causes for concern; rather, his colleagues, and non-Indigenous LGBTQ+ helping professionals working in downtown Toronto who are predominantly white, need to take active steps towards meaningfully engaging with Indigeneity and the land. Josh's queer-of-colour critique can be connected to Pride Toronto's land acknowledgment fail in 2019 insofar as the responsibility to acknowledge and thank the land should not rest onto the backs of Indigenous peoples to *do* the decolonizing work. Josh's narrative provides the context to consider how queers of colour are working towards understanding the struggles of Indigenous peoples and provides an opportunity to consider the depths of action required of white helping professionals in addressing the historical legacy of white settler colonialism in Canada (in which their queer organizations are firmly embedded).

Robert, a 32-year-old, white, queer, trans man who works as a health coordinator at a healthcare organization, illustrated how discussions of the land can often be empty:

> I think twice about what [this gesture] actually does when we open a conference or we open a discussion and somebody who is not a white settler says – but who's also not Native – says: "I'd like to thank the people who are lending us our land." It creates some sort of level of recognition in the room. But then some people just roll their eyes. It is like recycling – it makes us all feel better while it's actually still destroying the planet. (02/07/13, Transcript 13, p. 10, Toronto, ON)

Robert's narrative illustrates that queer organizations – specifically helping professionals of colour – are taking appropriate steps to adequately name the land as contested and "thank" Indigenous nations for the land. While these land acknowledgments do create some sense of recognition, some audience members typically "roll their eyes" in reaction to such a gesture. Concerning, as part of Robert's story, are the audience members' reactions of rolling their eyes at those who are doing the thanking – a response to viewing the land that they call home as unseeded, making the contemporary colonial realities Indigenous nations experience real. Robert's narrative also provides the context to consider how thanking Indigenous peoples for the land within the context of queer organizations may not be sufficient (referring back to Pride Toronto's 2019 land acknowledgment), inadequately addressing the disparities LGBTQ2S+ Indigenous peoples experience as a result of ongoing genocide and white settler colonialism.

The inclusion of Indigenous peoples within normatively white queer organizations typically occurs through white LGBTQ+ providers asserting their power and control over Indigenous peoples and communities through the guise of methods and models of inclusion. The whiteness of queer organizations is made to appear through some of the criticism offered by Josh. And despite this criticism, white LGBTQ+ helping professionals are reinscribing the project of sexual modernity as a project of settler colonial whiteness – further disconnecting the pressing concerns of BIPOC within queer organizations while also ensuring that the whiteness of the institutional walls is uninterrogated. While it is clear that white settler colonialism continues to constrain how Indigenous peoples can be meaningfully included within queer organizations, the stories below provide a more detailed account as to how Indigenous exclusion manifests. In particular, I take up the stories of white LGBTQ+ helping professionals as deflections of responsibility – as justifications for helping professionals not to include or address Indigeneity within their respective queer organizations.

Deflections of Responsibility

Some of the participant stories demonstrated how white LGBTQ+ helping professionals can remain complicit in white settler colonialism through acts of deflection. Ronald, a 32-year-old, white, gay, cisgender man who volunteers at a few organizations, talked with me about his uncertainty around knowing how queer organizations could be culturally appropriate and relevant for Indigenous service users.

> Q: Do you have Aboriginal service users at your agency?
> A: I do not know if I know enough about the specific needs of Aboriginal peoples who are accessing community services. I would hope that the shape that they would take would be one that represents those very specific needs. I am sure a lot of it would look very much the same. (02/09/13, Transcript 14, pp. 6–7, Toronto, ON)

Ronald illustrated that he does not have enough knowledge of the "specific needs" of Indigenous peoples in Canada to be able to imagine queer organizations differently. Although Ronald indicated that he does not have the appropriate or necessary knowledge of Indigenous peoples and their needs, he was able to articulate his feeling that the organization's overall structure would not need to change significantly in meeting those needs. In his expression of "not knowing," Ronald's narrative acts as a deflection of his responsibility in ongoing white settler colonialism and incites white settler innocence in Indigenous peoples' ongoing experiences of genocide. His narrative provides an opportunity to consider his and others' complicity in ongoing white settler colonial projects through a seemingly innocent admission regarding not having enough knowledge.

Similarly, Aaron, a 24-year-old, white, queer, cisgender man who works as a volunteer at a youth organization, discussed his trepidation around engaging with Indigeneity within the queer work he does. As he shared with me:

> If something comes up that I can read or educate myself on, it [Aboriginal issues] is always something that I try to tackle. It is also something that I would feel ... is an experience that I definitely could not describe in all of the complications that come with it. I am not close to anyone who identifies as Aboriginal or who has come from that background so it is not even something I can say that I know someone who has had this experience. It is something that I really am interested in and also that I am hesitant, completely hesitant to speak to. (04/23/13, Transcript 36, p. 5, Toronto, ON)

Aaron talked about his hesitation in speaking to Indigenous issues within the work he does. Although he works to educate himself, due to identifying as white he is uncomfortable with taking on Indigenous issues. Aaron also spoke of the lack of connection he has to Indigenous peoples within his personal life, which, in his estimation, is another reason why he is uncomfortable with addressing and including Indigenous content in his work. Aaron's narrative illustrates an active manifestation of innocence and complicity in white settler colonialism, particularly in his exclusion of Indigeneity as an appropriate topic of discussion for himself and within the work that he does. Not speaking to or addressing Indigeneity can easily naturalize the notion that Indigenous peoples only exist in the past – and, if they are seen to be present, their existences become unworthy of meaningful inclusion and disconnected from white queer organizations, as argued in Chapter 4.

In addressing the silencing of Indigenous content within queer organizations, Lisa, a 46-year-old, mixed-race, lesbian, cisgender woman who works as a newcomer-service coordinator at a large organization, spoke to the fact that people of colour, when accessing newcomer services more generally, are rarely educated on Indigenous issues. As she shared:

> When I first came to Canada I knew nothing about Aboriginal folks. Most of what I learned sort of by the way and to this day if you were to ask me to speak to the difference between Metis for instance and Inuit I would not know what you are talking about. I educated myself. As a newcomer, it is

safe for me to say that there are not many programs that taught me about
who was here before I was here. (01/15/13, Transcript 9, p. 1, Toronto, ON)

Within the context of her own experiences and as a queer, mixed-race
helping professional providing services for LGBTQ+ immigrants and/
or people of colour, Lisa pointed out that when she landed in Canada
she did not have a strong understanding of Indigenous peoples here
and, as a result, had to educate herself. While Lisa is merely a consumer
of immigration policy, we cannot deny that the forces of white settler
colonialism seep into immigration policy, making this seeming erasure
of Indigenous peoples ever more real. As Lisa illustrated, white queer
organizations do not adequately educate newcomers about Indigeneity, let alone about the effects of white settler colonialism in Canada.
Upon coming to this realization of Indigenous exclusion and erasure
within queer organizations, Lisa spoke with me about taking it upon
herself, in the work that she does, to provide LGBTQ+ service users of
colour with more information surrounding 2-Spiritedness. Lisa chooses
to include 2-Spiritedness within her workshops so that LGBTQ+ service users of colour cannot claim that they do not know the Indigenous
peoples here in Canada.

Finally, Candy, a 27-year-old, South Asian, genderqueer person who
works as a student intern at a large not for profit, illustrated that a
desire to include Indigenous peoples remains among white LGBTQ+
helping professionals and in the normatively white queer organizations at which they work. As they explained:

> I think we need to talk about colonialistic [sic] intent … moving program-
> ming toward what the colonialistic queers want … I think Aboriginal spe-
> cific programming can be great [but] I wonder what the place would be of
> [organization name removed]? I think the knee jerk reaction for us is '"yes,
> we have to, we have to do that because of inclusion and all of the other."
> Yet, as a QPOC [queer person of colour] I would say that sometimes the
> deal is that you give money to places that are already doing work with
> 2-Spirited people. There is 2-Spirits. But, 2-Spirits has no funding, they
> have no money, and this is the most highly funded LGBT organization in
> the world. (01/15/13, Transcript 8, p. 11, Toronto, ON)

Candy's narrative illustrates how there is often a desire coming from
white LGBTQ+ helping professionals to invite diversity and difference
into queer organizations. For normatively white queer organizations,
the inclusion of Indigenous peoples would make the organization
appear more inclusive. However, Candy also directed such a notion of

inclusivity towards a "colonialistic intent" that subsumes Indigenous difference within queer organizations and queer difference generally in Canada. Candy thus offered a queer-of-colour critique to queer organizations that would not require Indigenous peoples accessing services to do the work, suggesting that organizations such as the one they work for can provide smaller Indigenous-led organizations like 2-Spirits with more money better to serve their population. Instead of including for the sake of including, Candy suggested that the best way to aid Indigenous peoples is to support already-existing organizations that are financially struggling. Candy's narrative points to the barriers posed to normatively white queer organizations and its providers insofar as endeavours of solidarity aim to bring Indigeneity into an already normatively white system. Providing financial support to smaller Indigenous-led organizations would, in effect, challenge the normativity of white settler colonialism embedded within queer organizations.

The narratives offered by the research participants provide a context to consider how white LGBTQ+ helping professionals can deflect their responsibility in white supremacist and settler colonial processes, practices, and projects, all of which their queer organizations can normalize and sustain. The structure of queer organizations warrants further investigation – as a structure that condones Indigenous difference being included and yet simultaneously excluded. Some LGBTQ+ helping professionals of colour showed how their practices within queer organizations work towards challenging and rupturing the normativity of whiteness within queer organizations. I argue that larger processes and practices of white settler multiculturalism in Canada encourage white LGBTQ+ helping professionals to invite difference into queer organizations while effectively erasing it. As such, white helping professionals are often scripted into (often unknowingly) sustaining the logic of white settler colonialism through their attempts to foster inclusivity and diversity within queer organizations. As a result, I call attention to the innocence of white LGBTQ+ helping professionals as an act of deflection that diverts much-needed attention away from an analysis of white settler colonialism within the context of queer organizations.

A New Future?: Practicing Decolonization in Queer Organizations

In light of the very real ways in which white settler colonialism comes to elevate the concerns of white LGBTQ+ peoples and uphold the power of the normatively white organizations that they work within, I suggest that decolonization can be practised within queer organizations in Toronto, across Canada, and globally. Decolonization, as a means to end white settler colonialism's grip in Indigenous communities, means, for social work and other helping professions, a radical divestment in their current organization and operation. It also means that all helping professionals might have to give up their privilege (and even their jobs!) in order to work against existing white settler colonialism that social work readily sustains. For Deborah Barndt and Laura Reinsborough (2010), decolonization is: "a process of acknowledging the history of colonialism; working to undo the effects of colonialism; striving to unlearn habits, attitudes, and behaviours that continue to perpetuate colonialism; and challenging and transforming institutional manifestations of colonialism" (p. 161). At first glance, it seems like a useful endeavour to take on this approach; however, Barndt and Reinsborough's understanding of decolonization can, if utilized uncritically, erase Indigenous peoples and the land on which settler colonialism violently impedes.

For Qwo-Li Driskill (2010), decolonization addresses the "ongoing, radical resistance against colonialism that includes struggles for land, redress, self-determination, healing historical trauma, cultural continuance, and reconciliation" (p. 69). Driskill's understanding of decolonization moves beyond individual actions in order to address how we all can centre the radical resistance of colonialism and its violent effects inflicted upon Indigenous peoples and communities. For Harsha Walia (2013), "decolonization is a generative and prefigurative process whereby we create the conditions in which we want to live and the social relations we wish to have – for ourselves *and* everyone else" (p. 274; emphasis in original). Walia argues that decolonization occurs both on imaginative and material levels; whereby we all, by virtue of our connections to the land (Turtle Island), can challenge the hegemonic power structures (including the organizations for which we work) as one way to work towards effectively ending the global oppression that derides Indigenous self-determination and sovereignty. For Rosemary Nagy (2013), a practice of decolonization acts to "support and reinforce more acute, immediate processes of healing and renewal while also keeping justice in the foreground as a condition of 'never again' inflicting oppression and violence on [Indigenous peoples]" (p. 72). Working towards decolonization within the particular context of queer organizations has both rewards and consequences. For white LGBTQ+ helping professionals, this move towards addressing longstanding white settler colonialism both within the institution and within the previously mentioned evocations of (white) queerness is fraught with difficulty and discomfort.

A practice of decolonization, however, can result in slow but growing changes to larger institutional and societal practices – from which even helping professionals and organizations can benefit. At an institutional level, queer organizations can begin to create meaningful partnerships with Indigenous LGBTQ2S+ organizations; this might mean filtering existing resources and funds to Indigenous-led organizations and engaging in partnerships that do away with conventional power structures that privilege white settlers. These partnerships – ones that are founded on a coalitional politic, addressed in detail in the conclusion, which addresses the survival and resilience of Indigenous peoples and nations – should reflect a deep desire on the part of non-Indigenous LGBTQ+ helping professionals to work on (at both interpersonal and institutional levels) actively dismantling the white settler colonial conditions that continue to shape queer organizations. It is in this way that decolonization can provide an opportunity to move away from the discursive regimes of white settler multiculturalism and invite possibility, potential, and nuance into an already broken system.

Simultaneously, we can look at the subversive actions of LGBTQ+ people of colour, such as Josh, Lisa, and Candy, as challenging and transcending both white supremacy and settler colonialism within normatively white queer organizations as already-existing attempts to decolonize. Here, white LGBTQ+ peoples can learn from the risks that LGBTQ+ people of colour are taking within queer organizations and begin to take their active steps to ensure that the death and disappearance of Indigenous peoples, communities, and nations is halted. For white LGBTQ+ helping professionals, a practice of decolonization might start with opportunities on individual levels to know, unlearn, give up, or in some ways realize their roles in white settler colonialism to think and act differently. Within the white walls of queer organizations, this might mean naming white supremacy and settler colonialism within the programming, services, and educational initiatives offered – a risky move since this would likely decrease the amount of (government and private) funding accumulated through private and public donors. And we saw how this naming of white supremacy impacted the private funds available to Pride Toronto in 2018 – putting them in a financial deficit.

In the long term, a practice of decolonization might mean that the entirety of queer organizations is to be challenged, reworked, and possibly dismantled. Yet, until that time comes, moving towards decolonization ensures that non-Indigenous LGBTQ+ helping professionals take risks and make active attempts to decolonize their work so that the power and consequence of white settler colonialism can be named and worked against. A practice of decolonization can be imagined as a process and an outcome so that non-Indigenous LGBTQ+ helping professionals can start to consider how their everyday investments in LGBTQ2S+ identities and queer organizations can be challenged, as an avenue to pave the way for real change and to no longer place the sole responsibility to address white settler colonialism onto the backs of Indigenous peoples.

Conclusion: Building Decolonial Alliances and Working towards Queer Coalitions across Difference

Coalition work is not work done in your home. Coalition work has to be done in the streets. And it is some of the most dangerous work you can do. And you shouldn't look for comfort. Some people will come to a coalition and they rate the success of the coalition on whether or not they feel good when they get there. They're not looking for a coalition; they're looking for a home! (Reagon, 1983, p. 359)

I am not willing to embrace every queer as my marginalized political ally. In the same way, I do not assume that shared racial, gender, and/or class position or identity guarantees or produces similar political commitments. (Cohen, 1997, p. 458)

The narratives of the non-Indigenous LGBTQ+ research participants within this book provide an avenue for queer institutions and organizations in downtown Toronto to be seen as a white settler colonial structures that produce Indigenous peoples as "problems" who become unworthy of care; simultaneously, Indigenous peoples become engulfed within a larger white settler culture, in which queer organizations in Toronto reside, that embrace white settler multiculturalism and cultures of diversity. The reflections made in this book are an invitation and call to action on the part of all non-Indigenous peoples across Canada and a specific reminder to non-Indigenous LGBTQ+ helping professionals, organizers, activists, and community members to take an active role in transforming their current contributions to queer organizations so that the white supremacist and settler colonial violence inflicted upon BIPOC can be named and worked against. Non-Indigenous LGBTQ+ helping professionals are invited (often unknowingly) to participate in sustaining the white settler colonial project in their imaginations of a queer (settler) future, and, as such, queer organizations in Toronto cannot escape its history. It is my goal is to invite non-Indigenous helping professionals generally to critically investigate their helping orientations – insofar as these frameworks, often operationalized as being culturally competent, multicultural, or socially just, can situate the helper in a power-over relationship with the Other whom they are required to help, save, and bring into modernity. In centralizing Indigenous decolonization and the analysis of white settler colonialism within work done within queer organizations, new relationships with Indigenous peoples, helping professionals, and their nations/communities can be developed to subvert larger white settler colonialism in Canada.

However, this will not be an easy task to undertake, since it will require white helping professionals, who are overrepresented in queer organizations in Toronto and other urban centres, to do away with the helping imperative (Heron, 2007) therein; within their helping roles and work life, white helping professionals can begin to challenge the ways LGBTQ2S+ identities and experiences are taken up and given meaning within queer organizations. White settler descendants have the responsibility to uncover and dig deep into how we contribute (often unknowingly) to white settler colonial projects to repair such historical wrongdoings. Such repairs would lead to taking action against how modern LGBTQ2S+ identities and queer formations continue to repudiate Indigenous life and erase any possibilities for Indigenous decolonization across Canada.

The impetus of this book is to understand the depth and degree to which non-Indigenous LGBTQ+ helping professionals might better support the existing and future decolonial efforts of Indigenous peoples and nations – within queer organizations in Toronto and beyond. For many non-Indigenous helping professionals, their investment in diversity and dialogue rests within a professional mandate that "promote[s] social justice," as stated by the Canadian Association for Social Workers, National Association for Social Workers, and National Organization for Human Services, or embedded within the mission of the organization as per the 519, which works within an "anti-oppressive social justice framework." Importantly, whether through the professionalization of queerness or an organization's mission statement, helping professionals are encouraged and ethically mandated to work towards and practise social justice; however, this commitment seems to be fluid among individuals themselves and various organizations, proving that the term *social justice* can ensure contradictory massages and meanings as per the narratives of the research participants shared throughout this book.

White LGBTQ+ helping professionals whom I have spoken with indicated that they are in support of equality, diversity, and inclusion within their queer organization to expand the services and supports that they offer; however, it seems that, while there is an investment in social justice, the imagined LGBTQ2S+ subject, who is deserving of help or care, remains white. Rarely, if at all, are the imaginings of the work done within queer organizations, or the service users who are deserving of help or care, Indigenous. These Indigenous service users wholeheartedly are required to make use of specialized services that Linklater (2014) suggests are there to support Indigenous peoples' health, well-being, and healing. Consequently, this contradictory orientation queer organizations produce seems to be firmly embedded within LGBTQ2S+ identity politics – making the imaginings of working within queer organizations and doing queer work always negotiated through the system of white settler colonialism.

Simultaneously, while the roots of queer organizations are tied deeply to discourses of human rights, diversity, and multiculturalism whereby to engage in social change, non-Indigenous LGBTQ+ helping professionals are required to invest in the queer institution despite knowing its ongoing failures to decolonize. Instead, what occurs within these queer organizations is a deep, routine reorientation to white settler normativity – a normativity, I argue, that is saturated in the neoliberalization of queerness and the white settler colonial industry of helping work itself (Greensmith, 2015). While it might be awfully simple to recommend a complete eradication of queer organizations, they are, unfortunately (or fortunately) not going anywhere. With more energy directed at encouraging, fuelling, and fostering the development of LGBTQ2S+ peoples as peoples and the flourishing of their (our?) communities, as well as the focus on same-but-different inclusionary politics, many queer organizations in Toronto are continuing to take advantage of the current political moment and are thriving. These queer organizations are at once utilizing the discourses the state mobilizes to foster inclusion and diversity and working to challenge the very discourses to magnify specific issues of concern (often localized within the context of trauma or pain as noted in Chapter 5). To amplify this disquiet, queer organizations, with their power and influence, continue to develop partnerships (which are highly encouraged through funding bodies) with ethnospecific/Indigenous organizations to address persistent gaps within the organization. For queer organizations to push against (and queer) the power of professionalization, I look to the development of alliances, solidarity, and coalitions within and beyond the context of the helping professions.

Beyond Organizations: Building Alliances and Engaging Solidarity Work

Idle No More was launched in December of 2012 by Sylvia McAdam, Jess Gordon, Nina Wilson, and Sheelah Mclean (The Kino-nda-niimi Collective, 2014). The Idle No More movement invites non-Indigenous peoples, within their differing investments in and relationships to Canadian citizenship, to place themselves in relationships with Indigenous peoples and work towards challenging white settler colonial domination in Canada. Non-Indigenous peoples are encouraged to act with Indigenous peoples, support decolonial resistance, and bring attention to the white settler colonial conditions in place in contemporary Canada. Idle No More emerged as a means to bring necessary attention to

1 The repeal of significant sections of the Canadian federal government's omnibus legislation (Bills C-38 and C-45) and specifically parts relating to the exploitation of the environment, water, and First Nations territories.
2 The stabilization of emergency situations in First Nations communities, such as Attawapiskat, accompanied by an honest, collaborative approach to addressing issues relating to Indigenous communities and self-sustainability, land, education, housing, and healthcare, among others.
3 A commitment to a mutually beneficial nation-to-nation relationship between Canada, First Nations (status and nonstatus), Inuit, and Metis communities based on the spirits and intent of treaties and a recognition of inherent and shared rights and responsibilities as equal and unique partners. A large part of this includes an end to the unilateral legislative and policy process Canadian governments have favoured to amend the Indian Act. (The Kino-nda-niimi Collective, 2014, p. 22)

The Idle No More movement addresses the ongoing white settler colonial violence Indigenous peoples experience, as well as the broken treaties and inviting rejuvenating relationships to the land. The movement also invites non-Indigenous peoples (regardless of how they identify) to consider their relationships to land and the treaties in Canada to work together as allies in challenging the existing oppressions Indigenous peoples, communities, and nations experience.

In response to Idle No More inviting non-Indigenous peoples to organize and engage in decolonial relations, "Skills for Solidarity" (Skills for Solidarity, 2014) emerged. The Skills for Solidarity network attempted to expand opportunities for non-Indigenous and Indigenous peoples in Canada to build relationships by "provid[ing] an overview of what it looks like to renew the relationship between nations and continue to work together on a variety of campaigns and issues" (n.p.). As a first step, the Skills for Solidarity network provided an opportunity to develop a dialogue between Indigenous and non-Indigenous peoples in Canada as a way to renew relationships and work collectively in support of Indigenous decolonization. The Idle No More movement has also provided an avenue for white settlers to question their benevolence in sustaining Canada's settler colonial history and to showcase how non-Indigenous people can collectively organize with Indigenous peoples to challenge the dominant narratives of multiculturalism that continue to erase Canada's white supremacist and settler colonial history.

Looking to the organizing efforts of Indigenous women, girls, and LGBTQ2S+ peoples in addressing longstanding gendered and sexual violence, Belcourt (2018) discusses the goals and principles of Walking With Our Sisters, noting: "everything we do flows from these principles:

- All who attend are equal. All are welcome.
- The memorial in each community is Indigenous led.
- Practice kindness, gentleness, patience, and love.
- We are all volunteers. No one is paid. No profits are made" (p. xiii).

The organizing efforts of Walking With Our Sisters puts into perspective the potentiality of engaging in alliance and solidarity work with Indigenous peoples, which occurs out of a desire to challenge historical and contemporary manifestations of white settler colonialism. Indeed, the premise behind the alliance or solidarity work done always centres Indigenous peoples and their humanity, while also disavowing the ways many professional organizations and associations have coopted Indigenous struggles and Indigenous decolonization under the auspice of helping.

A connected, yet different response to the professionalization of care is the example of disabled peoples' community care collectives and webs. These initiatives emerged out of disability justice movements that engage disability as a multi-issue politic, with a centralized focus on equity, and focuses on the liberation of disabled people and their communities (Piepzna-Samarashinha, 2018). For Piepzna-Samarashinha (2018), care collectives or webs challenge the existing structures within which disabled peoples are placed and made to matter through "'official' disability accommodation" (p. 36) or when "able-bodied people begrudging [sic] 'helping' us" (p. 49). Piepzna-Samarashinha (2018) notes that care collectives or webs act as cross-disability solidarity, where predominantly disabled people of colour are helping and supporting each other and caring for each other outside of for- or nonprofit organizations that rely on the medical-industrial complex to define and name disability: "Crip-on-crip support is awesome! Often, after a lifetime of ableist able-bodied people providing shitty or abusive care and assuming that we're not able to do anything ourselves, disabled people caring for each other can be a place of deep healing" (p. 65). The organizing efforts, alliances, and solidarity among disabled people, Indigenous peoples, and their allies may be where possibilities lie to meaningfully address the power of white settler colonialism within helping organizations and professions.

Coalitions: Beyond Identity Politics

What is to follow, I argue, is a radical rethinking of engaging queer organizations and communities through their difference and not their assumed similarities – a difference that is produced and imagined outside of LGBTQ2S+ identity politics. As Cathy Cohen (1997) argues, this production of queer difference, couched within identity politics, continues to be exclusionary to many poor Black women who will never, cannot, or choose not to occupy the category of *queer*. For queer organizations and communities in Canada to work effectively towards a decolonial future, I suggest that it would need to start by centring the struggles of BIPOC, who are made to be queer through institutions of state violence. As queer institutions and the seeming professionals who run them, they have a responsibility to unlearn, give up, or otherwise resist the oppressive regimes and systems from which they benefit.

This is no easy task. And such an orientation could be an end of queer organizations as we currently know them. Yet this end, and the actions that result, would be operationalized through the understanding that the overall need for such organizations is no longer – what would it mean for care collectives to emerge in local queer/disability communities? In other words, the actions and interventions made possible within queer organizations and the work of helping professionals would actively work towards a more just world – a justice that is not mandated by their professional body, rather, this justice that is to be imagined by BIPOC communities. And a justice that will always organically change, through which the necessities of the most marginalized peoples are met. As Reagon (1989) notes this is neither simple nor cushy; acts of coalition-building work to unravel existing inequalities and structures of oppression within social movements and organizations while simultaneously working to challenge the status quo.

Within the context of queer organizations in Toronto and across Canada, working towards a coalition would mean not just paying lip service to existing inequalities Indigenous people experience or producing a land acknowledgment statement like Pride Toronto did in 2019 but would look to actively engage the existing alliances among and solidarity work of BIPOC (even if that work happens alongside them and/or their organization). As hooks (1988) and Jones (1999) note, despite the good intentions of white women, to support the existing endeavours of BIPOC they must do away with producing BIPOC as vessels of knowledge; instead, non-Indigenous helping professionals, who occupy privileged and complicit positions, have access to existing data documenting histories of violence inflicted upon BIPOC, case studies on the historical and contemporary wrongdoings, professional documents regarding working with and supporting marginalized communities, and other entry points that allow helping professionals, activists, and organizers to engage directly with the writings of BIPOC without burdening them.

And, while these materials are available, the only way non-Indigenous helping professionals can engage in and support social justice struggles and Indigenous reconciliation is to actively and persistently do the decolonial work and challenge white settler colonialism – even if that means resisting or overthrowing the queer organization and professions in which they work and which they value. The challenges lie in the contradictions between working within a queer organization designed to help Others, effectively bringing them into modernity, while simultaneously working within the funding constraints placed upon organizations. Simultaneously, there remains a central problem: LGBTQ2S+ identity, which is produced and legitimized by the state, is often used to prop up white settler colonial logics and institutions. The concern many of the research participants highlight is the inability for white LGBTQ+ helping professionals to understand their work as contributing to white settler colonialism, or, if they are understanding of the severity, they believe that their actions or good intentions will set them apart from those "bad people" – a misguided approach that fails to consider their complicity in white settler colonial struggles.

I will end not with a formula, a checklist, or a series of approaches to decolonize queer organizations. Instead, I offer the words of Gloria Anzaldua (2009), who notes, "nothing happens in the 'real' world unless it first happens in the images in our heads" (p. 310). That is, our complacency or in/action begins within our imaginations – we must be able to imagine the world differently so that we can act differently. And we are all differently situated in our roles as helping professionals, organizers, activists, and community members: we may volunteer, be an executive director, be on a research team, and/or access programs or services. Important in our difference among each other is our responsibility to Indigenous peoples, communities, and nations; we must be able to imagine anew so to work against the persistent and long-lasting impact of anti-Indigenous racism and Indigenous genocide normalized within queer organizations and communities, which routinely latch onto state articulations of queerness. It is only then, in our action, that we can deploy resistance tactics that trouble and push against queer organizations that are not serving BIPOC well.

In the following list, I offer a series of questions for helping professionals to begin to take action and engage in the making of (queer) decolonial coalitions. I suggest that non-Indigenous helping professionals, activists, organizers, and anyone else reading this book start to ask themselves and their organizations the following questions:

1 How might I (or my family) benefit from white supremacy and settler colonialism in Canada or globally?
2 What kinds of action-oriented strategies could I employ to reduce, challenge, and/or subvert the white supremacy and settler colonialism from which I benefit?
3 What kinds of organizations are already supporting the particular needs of BIPOC?
   i How might I (and my organization) get involved and/or support them?
4 If Indigenous peoples and organizations do not request or desire support from non-Indigenous peoples, how might non-Indigenous helping professionals start to incorporate an analysis of white settler colonialism within their practices, organizational structures, and professions?
5 How might queer organizations be more safe, inclusive, and inviting of Indigenous peoples and foster a space for Indigenous requests for service, coalition, and collaboration?
6 Why do you (or your organization) desire to include Indigeneity in your practice and/or organization?
7 Are these particular inclusionary measures intended for Indigenous service users?
   i If so, how would you ensure that you and/or your organization incorporate Indigenous ways of knowing respectfully?
   ii If not, why make the active attempt to include Indigeneity?

8 Have you consulted written materials for Indigenous-led organizations, activists, organizers, and/or scholars about the particular ways of knowing you wish to incorporate in your practice (e.g., healing circles, tobacco, smudging)?
9 Is the particular inclusion of Indigenous ways of knowing supported by your organization?
10 Should Indigenous peoples be thanked for their land and generosity?
11 What kinds of effects occur when non-Indigenous peoples thank Indigenous peoples for their land and generosity?
12 Is thanking Indigenous peoples for their land and generosity, and/or naming the land as contested, enough of an action?
13 In naming the land as contested, or thanking Indigenous peoples for their land, how does such an act support and/or act toward Indigenous decolonization?
14 What would it mean for you to leave Turtle Island (Canada) and give the land back to Indigenous peoples?
  i If this is unimaginable, how instead might you meaningfully support and act responsibly toward BIPOC, whose lives are constrained by white settler colonialism?
15 Why do you and/or your organization feel as though you need to hear or witness the voices of Indigenous peoples to move forward on making changes to service provision and/or programming?
  i Do you engage with qualitative and/or community-based research that has already articulated the particular needs of urban, rural, or reserve-based Indigenous peoples?
16 Within your respective organization, position, and profession, what concerns have Indigenous peoples you have interacted with already voiced?
17 What (if any) initiatives exist in other organizations that support Indigenous service users?

These sets of questions are important to consider, insofar as the inclusionary endeavours mobilized by non-Indigenous helping professionals may not necessarily add anything new to the already well-developed pool of resources developed by Indigenous peoples, activists, organizers, and academics and indeed may deflect much-needed analysis of white settler colonialism within the organizations for which we work. It is these questions that I have found helpful to ask myself so that I start to meaningfully centre and practise Indigenous decolonization within my work to build meaningful coalitions and relationships centred on our differences. I hope that this book and the aforementioned questions spark more questioning and more opportunities for non-Indigenous peoples – whether helping professionals, activists, organizers, or academics – to consider how queer organizations, queer professionals, and queer helping work more generally can be challenged insofar as they operate from a white settler colonial historical legacy that maintains and naturalizes the logics of Indigenous genocide used to erase, manage, and contain BIPOC. For how purposeful is queerness if, as a tactic for social change, it remains exclusionary?

Notes

1. Understanding the Historical and Contemporary Realities of (White) Queer Organizations in Toronto

1 "The Body Politic was the leading community-based, gay liberationist magazine, publishing 135 issues between 1971 and 1987. Those involved in the paper's development describe it as a radical that 'evolved gradually into a Toronto-centred community service newspaper with a strong national outreach.' The Body Politic addressed issues of discrimination, human rights and community development" (Nash, 2006, p. 6).

2 I only use "Aboriginal" within my reporting on the in-depth interviews conducted for this book project. The term "Aboriginal," unfortunately, is a common trope used within everyday speech to mark, differentiate, and Other Indigenous peoples in what is now known as Canada. In using "Aboriginal," I acknowledge the ways in which the term was created by the settler colonial Canadian nation state (Alfred, 2005).

3 *Convention refugees* can be defined as "people who are outside their home country or the country where they normally live, and who are unwilling to return because of a well-founded fear of persecution based on: race; religion; political opinion; nationality; or membership in a particular social group, such as women or people of a particular sexual orientation" ("Determine your," 2012).

2. "We Had the Rainbow:" Queer Organizations and the Desire for White Settler Multiculturalism

1 The cultural mosaic metaphor refers to the preservation of national, cultural, and ethnic difference. And, while criticism regarding Canadian nationhood remains assimilatory, multiculturalism utilizes this metaphor as a way to sustain political and ideological differences from that of its neighbour: The United States of America.

2 The American *melting pot* is a metaphor used to refer to the fusion of national, cultural, and ethnic differences into one homogeneous national identity. The melting pot often refers to an assimilation process that requires immigrants to extinguish their difference.

3 Ryan self-identified as white at the beginning of the interview; yet, as we started to develop a relationship and connect, he shared that he recently found out that he had Indigenous ancestry. He did not share anything else with regard to this finding and did not indicate that this had impacted him or his understandings of the work he does.

4 2-Spirited People of the First Nations is a not-for-profit organization that works to support Indigenous peoples who are HIV-positive, LGBTQ+, and/or 2-Spirited in the greater Toronto area by providing education, one-on-one counseling, and other support services.

5 *2-Spirit* is an English term used by Indigenous peoples to "reflect their gendered and sexual differences, as well as their connections to Indigeneity" (Greensmith & Giwa 2013, p. 130).

5. A Call to Action: Queerness, Complicity, and Deflecting Responsibility

1 The Native Youth Sexual Health Network is a nationwide not-for-profit organization that is youth-led. This organization works towards addressing the interlocking inequalities of racism, colonialism, and heteropatriarchy in Indigenous people's lives – trying to attend to the urban/rural divide present within contemporary social work and organizations for Indigenous peoples and sexual health.

References

519 Church Street Community Centre. *The 519 church street community centre.* Retrieved from: https://www.the519.org

Absolon, K., & Willett, C. (2005). Putting ourselves forward: Location in Aboriginal research. In L. Brown & S. Strega (Eds.), *Research as resistance: Critical, indigenous & anti-oppressive approaches* (pp. 97–126). Canadian Scholars Press.

Ahmed, S. (2000). *Strange encounters: Embodied others in post-colonialism.* Routledge.

Ahmed, S. (2012). Speaking about racism. In *On being included: Racism and diversity in institutional life* (pp. 141–72). Duke University Press.

AIDS Committee of Toronto. (2021). *Mission, vision, and core commitments.* https://www.actoronto.org/about-act/our-organization/vision,-mission -core-commitments

Alfred, T. (2005). *Wasáse: Indigenous pathways of action and freedom.* Broadview Press.

Alfred, T. (2009). *Peace, power, righteousness: An Indigenous manifesto* (2nd ed.). Oxford University Press.

Amadahy, Z., & Lawrence, B. (2009). Indigenous peoples and Black people in Canada: Settlers or allies? In A. Kempf (Ed.), *Breaching the colonial contract: Anti-colonialism in the US and Canada* (pp. 105–36). Springer.

Amnesty International. (October 2004). *Stolen sisters: A human rights response to discrimination and violence against Indigenous women in Canada.* https:// www.amnesty.ca/sites/amnesty/files/amr200032004enstolensisters.pdf

Anderson, K. (2000). Our human relations. In *A recognition of being: Reconstructing Native womanhood* (pp. 158–79). Sumach Press.

Anderson, K., Campbell, M., & Belcourt, C. (Eds.). (2018). *Keetsahnak/our missing and murdered Indigenous sisters.* University of Alberta Press.

Anzaldua, G. (2009). La conciencia de la mestiza. In R. Warhol-Down & D. Price Herndl (Eds.), *Feminisms redux: An anthology of literary theory and criticism* (pp. 303–13). Rutgers University Press.

Applebaum, B. (2011). *Being white, being good: White complicity, white moral responsibility, and social justice pedagogy* (pp. 179–202). Lexington Books.

Arriola, E. R. (1995). Faeries, marimachas, queens, and lezzies: The construction of homosexuality before the 1969 Stonewall Riots. *Columbia Journal of Gender and Law, 5*(1). https://doi.org/10.7916/cjgl.v5i1.2378

Azzam, R. (2011). *Multiculturalism and the contestation of holidays in schools.* [Unpublished master's thesis]. University of Toronto.

Badwall, H. (2013). *Can I be a good social worker? Racialized workers narrate their experiences with racism in every day practice.* [Unpublished doctoral dissertation]. University of Toronto.

Bannerji, H. (2000). *The dark side of the nation: Essays on multiculturalism, nationalism and gender.* Canadian Scholars' Press.

Barker, J. (2015). Indigenous feminisms. In J. A. Lucero, D. Turner, & D. L. VanCott (Eds.), *Handbook on Indigenous people's politics* (pp. 1–17). Oxford University Press.

Barker, J. (Ed.). (2017). *Critically sovereign: Indigenous gender, sexuality, and feminist studies.* Duke University Press.

Barndt, D., & Reinsborough, L. (2010). Decolonizing art, education, and research in the VIVA project. In L. Davis (Ed.), *Alliances: Re/envisioning Indigenous-non-Indigenous relationships* (pp. 158–77). University of Toronto Press.

Belcourt, C. (2018). Prologue: Waking dreams: Reflections on walking with our sisters. In K. Anderson, M. Campbell, & C. Belcourt (Eds.), *Keetsahnak/ our missing and murdered Indigenous sisters* (pp. xi–xvii). University of Alberta Press.

Bishop, A. (2002). Becoming an ally. In *Becoming an ally: Breaking the cycle of oppression in people* (pp. 109–22). Fernwood Publishing.

The Body Politic. (1972). *Ontario human rights code.* (No. 5). Canadian Gay and Lesbian Archives, Toronto, Ontario, Canada.

Brant, J. (2020, May 28). *Indigenous communities come together virtually during coronavirus despite barriers and inequities.* The Conversation. https://theconversation.com/indigenous-communities-come-together-virtually-during-coronavirus-despite-barriers-and-inequities-138601

Britzman, D. (1995). Is there a queer pedagogy? Or, stop reading straight. *Educational Theory, 45*(2), 151–65. https://doi.org/10.1111/j.1741-5446.1995.00151.x

Brown, W. (1995). Wounded attachments. In *States of injury: Power and freedom in late modernity* (pp. 52–76). Princeton University Press.

Byrd, J. A. (2011). *The transit of empire: Indigenous critiques of colonialism.* University of Minnesota Press.

Cain, R. (2002). Devoting ourselves, devouring each other. *Journal of Progressive Human Services, 13*(1), 93–113. DOI: 10.1300/J059v13n01_06

Canadian Blood Services. (2017a). *Men who have sex with men.* https://blood .ca/en/men-who-have-sex-men

Canadian Blood Services. (2017b). *Eligibility criteria for trans individuals.* https://blood.ca/en/eligibility-criteria-trans

Canadian Blood Services. (2017c). *The ABCs of eligibility.* https://blood.ca/en /blood/abcs-eligibility

Cannon, M. (1998). The regulation of First Nations sexuality. *The Canadian Journal of Native, xviii*(1), 1–18.

Cannon, M. (2012). Changing the subject in teacher education: Centering Indigenous, diasporic, and settler colonial relations. *Cultural and Pedagogical Inquiry, 4*(2), 21–37. DOI: https://doi.org/10.18733/C3KS3D

Cannon, M., & Sunseri, L. (2018). *Racism, colonialism, and indigeneity in Canada* (2nd ed.). Oxford University Press Canada.

Carbado, D. (2005). Privilege. In E. P. Johnson & M. G. Henderson (Eds.), *Black queer studies: A critical anthology.* (pp. 190–212). Duke University Press.

Casey, M. (2004). De-dyking queer space(s): Heterosexual female visibility in gay and lesbian spaces. *Sexualities, 7*(4), 446–61. https://doi.org/10.1177 /1363460704047062

Casey House. (2021). *Vision, mission and values.* https://www.caseyhouse.com /about-casey-house/casey-houses-values/

Catungal, J. P. (2013). Ethno-specific safe houses in the liberal contact zone: Race politics, place-making and the genealogies of the AIDS sector in global-multicultural Toronto. *ACME: An International E-Journal for Critical Geographies, 12*(2), 250–78. https://acme-journal.org/index.php/acme /article/view/962

CBC News. (2019, June 24). Pride Toronto apologizes for land acknowledgement that "failed to recognize" Indigenous peoples. https://www.cbc.ca/news /canada/toronto/pride-toronto-indigenous-land-acknowledgement-1.5188127

Centre for Addiction and Mental Health. (2021). *Rainbow Services (LGBTQ).* https://www.camh.ca/en/your-care/programs-and-services/ rainbow-services-lgbtq

Chazan, M., Helps, L., Stanley, A., & Thakkar, S. (2011). Introduction: Labours, lands, bodies. In M. Chazan, L. Helps, A. Stanley, & S. Thakkar (Eds.), *Home and native land: Unsettling multiculturalism in Canada.* Between the Lines.

City of Toronto. (2013, May 9). 2011 national household survey: Immigration, citizenship, place of birth, ethnicity, visible minorities, religion and Aboriginal peoples. *Backgrounder.* https://www.toronto.ca/wp-content

/uploads/2017/10/9793-2011-NHS-Backgrounder-Immigration-Citizenship
-Place-of-Birth-Ethnicity-Visible-Minorities-Religion-and-Aboriginal
-Peoples-.pdf

Clarke, J. (2010). The challenges of child welfare involvement for Afro-Caribbean Canadian families in Toronto. *Children and Youth Services Review,* *33*(2), 274–83. https://doi.org/10.1016/j.childyouth.2010.09.010

Cohen, C. J. (1997). Punks, bulldaggers and welfare queens: The radical potential of queer politics? *GLQ: A Journal of Lesbian and Gay Studies, 3*(4), 437–65. https://doi.org/10.1215/10642684-3-4-437

Coleman, D. (2006). *White civility and the literary project of English Canada.* University of Toronto Press.

Coulthard, G. (2007). Subjects of empire: Indigenous peoples and the politics of recognition in Canada. *Contemporary Political Theory, 6,* 437–60. https://doi.org/10.1057/palgrave.cpt.9300307

Cross T., Bazron, B., Dennis, K. & Isaacs, M. (1989). *Towards a culturally competent system of care* (Vol. 1). Georgetown University Child Development Center.

Czyzewski, K. (2011). Colonialism as a broader social determinant of health. *The International Indigenous Policy Journal, 2*(1). http://ir.lib.uwo.ca/iipj/vol2/iss1/5/

Day, R. (2000). *Multiculturalism and the history of Canadian diversity.* University of Toronto Press.

DiAngelo, R. (2011). White fragility. *The International Journal of Critical Pedagogy, 3*(3), 54–70. https://libjournal.uncg.edu/ijcp/article/view/249

DiAngelo, R. (2018). *White fragility: Why it's so hard for white people to talk about racism.* Beacon Press.

Dion, S. D. (2009). *Braiding histories: Learning from Aboriginal peoples' experiences and perspectives.* University of British Columbia Press.

Drable, L., & Ellason, M. J. (2012). Substance use disorders treatment for sexual minority women. *Journal of LGBT Issues in Counseling, 6*(4), 274–92. DOI: 10.1080/15538605.2012.726150

Drescher, J. (2015). Out of DSM: Depathologizing homosexuality. *Behavioral Sciences, 5*(4), 565–75. DOI: 10.3390/bs5040565

Driskill, Q. (2010). Doubleweaving Two-Spirit Critiques: Building Alliances between Native and Queer Studies. *GLQ, 16*(1–2): 69–92. DOI: https://doi.org/10.1215/10642684-2009-013

Driskill, Q., Finley, C., Gilley, B. J., & Morgensen, S. L. (2011). Introduction. In *Queer Indigenous studies: Critical interventions in theory, politics, and literature* (pp. 1–30). University of Arizona Press.

Dryden, O. (2010). Canadians denied: a queer diasporic analysis of the Canadian blood donor. *Atlantis, 34*(2), 77–84.

Eng, D. (2010). *The feeling of kinship: Queer liberalism and the racialization of intimacy.* Duke University Press.

Fellows, M. L., & Razack, S. (1997–8). The race to innocence: Confronting hierarchical relations among women. *Journal of Gender, Race and Justice, 1,* 335–52. https://scholarship.law.umn.edu/faculty_articles/274

Fish, J. (2007). Getting equal: The implications of new regulations to prohibit sexual orientation discrimination for health and social care. *Diversity in Health and Social Care, 4*(3), 221–8.

FitzGerald, M., & Rayter, S. (2012). *Queerly Canadian: An introductory reader in sexuality studies.* Canadian Scholars' Press.

Foucault, M. (1978). Part five: Right of death and power over life. In *The history of sexuality* (R. Hurley, Trans.). Vintage.

Francis, M. (2011). *Creative subversions: Whiteness, Indigeneity, and the national imaginary.* UBC Press.

Frankenberg, R. (1993). *White women, race matters: The social construction of whiteness.* Routledge.

Fraser, N. (2000). Rethinking recognition. *Left Review, 3,* 107–20. https://newleftreview.org/issues/ii3/articles/nancy-fraser-rethinking-recognition

Fujikane, C., & Okamura, J. Y. (2008). *Asian settler colonialism: From local governance to the habits of everyday life in Hawai'i.* University of Hawai'i Press.

Giwa, S., & Greensmith, C. (2012). Race relations and racism in the LGBTQ+ community of Toronto: Perceptions of gay and queer social helping professionals of color. *Journal of Homosexuality, 59*(2), 149–85. DOI: 10.1080/00918369.2012.648877

Gopinath, G. (2005). *Impossible desires: Queer diasporas and South Asian public cultures.* Durham, NC: Duke University Press.

Government of Canada. (2012a, March 7). *Discover Canada.* http://www.cic.gc.ca/english/resources/publications/discover/read.asp

Government of Canada. (2012b, October 26). *Who we are.* http://www.cic.gc.ca/english/resources/publications/discover/section-05.asp

Green, J. (2001). Canaries in the mines of citizenship: Indian women in Canada. *Canadian Journal of Political Science/Revue canadienne de science politique, 34*(4), 715–38. https://www.jstor.org/stable/3232880

Greensmith, C. (2012). Pathologizing Indigeneity in the Caledonia "crisis." *Canadian Journal of Disability Studies, 1*(2), 18–42. DOI: https://doi.org/10.15353/cjds.v1i2.41

Greensmith, C. (2015). Bathhouse encounters: Settler colonialism, volunteerism and Indigenous misrecognition. In C. Janzen, D. Jeffery, & K. Smith (Eds.), *Unraveling encounters: Ethics, knowledge, and resistance under neoliberalism* (pp. 95–125). Wilfrid Laurier University Press.

Greensmith, C., & Giwa, S. (2013). Challenging settler colonialism in contemporary queer politics: Settler homonationalism, Pride Toronto, and two-spirit subjectivities. *American Indian Culture and Research Journal, 37*(2), 129–48. https://doi.org/10.17953/aicr.37.2.p4q2r84l12735117

Greensmith, C., & King, B. (2020). "Queer as hell media": Affirming LGBTQ+ youth identity and building community in Metro Atlanta, Georgia. *Journal of LGBT Youth*, 1–18. DOI: 10.1080/19361653.2020.1829524

Greensmith, C., & Sheppard, L. (2018). At the age of twelve: Migrant children and the disruption of multicultural belonging. *Children & Society*, 32(4), 255–65. https://doi.org/10.1111/chso.12251

Gross, Z. (2015). (De)constructing whiteness, power, and 'Others' with access: International development and transnational interracial intimacies in East Africa. *Critical Race & Whiteness Studies*, 11(1), 1–19. https://acrawsa .org.au/wp-content/uploads/2017/09/255Gross2015111.pdf

Haig-Brown, C. (2009). Decolonizing diaspora. *Cultural and Pedagogical Inquiry*, 1(1), 4–21. DOI: https://doi.org/10.18733/C3H59V

Hamilton, C. J., & Mahalik, J. R. (2009). Minority stress, masculinity, and social norms predicting gay men's health risk behaviors. *Journal of Counseling Psychology*, 56(1), 132–41. https://doi.org/10.1037/a0014440

Hanhardt, C. B. (2013). *Safe space: Gay neighborhood history and the politics of violence.* Duke University Press.

Hargreaves, A. (2017). *Violence against Indigenous women: Literature, activism, resistance.* Wilfrid Laurier University Press.

Hassle Free Clinic. (n.d.). *About Hassle Free Clinic.* https://www.hasslefreeclinic. org/about

Heron, B. (2007). *Desire for development: Whiteness, gender, and the helping imperative.* Wilfred Laurier Press.

Hill-Collins, P. (2003). Toward a new vision: Race, class, and gender as categories of analysis and connection. In M. S. Kimmel & A. L. Ferber (Eds.), *Privilege: A reader* (pp. 331–48). Westview Press.

hooks, b. (1988). Talking back: Thinking feminist, thinking Black. South End Press.

hooks, b. (2003). *Teaching community: A pedagogy of hope.* Routledge.

Hughes, T. L. (2005). Alcohol use and alcohol-related problems among lesbians and gay men. *Annual Review of Nursing Research*, 23(1), 283–325. DOI: 10.1891/0739-6686.23.1.283

Hunt, S., & Holmes, C. (2015). Everyday decolonization: Living a decolonizing queer politics. *Journal of lesbian studies*, 19(2), 154–72. DOI: 10.1080/10894160.2015.970975

Hyde, C. A. (2018). Leading from below: Low-power actors as organizational change agents. *Human Service Organizations: Management, Leadership & Governance*, 42(1), 53–67. DOI: 10.1080/23303131.2017.1360229

Jafri, B. (2012). Privilege vs. complicity: People of colour and settler colonialism. *Federation for the Humanities and Social Sciences.* http://www.fedcan.ca/en/ blog/privilege-vs-complicity-people-colour-and-settler-colonialismx

Jafri, B. (2013). Desire, settler colonialism, and the racialized cowboy. *American Indian Culture and Research Journal, 37*(2), 73–86. https://doi.org/10.17953/aicr.37.2.n758545211525815

Jeffery, D. (2009). Meeting here and now: Reflections on racial and cultural difference in social work encounters. In S. Strega & Sohki Aski Esquao [Jeannine Carriere] (Eds.), *Walking this path together: Anti-racist and anti-oppressive child welfare practice* (pp. 45–61). Fernwood Publishing.

Jensen, B. (2012). *Reading classes: On culture and classism in America*. Cornell University Press.

Jones, A. (1999). The limits of cross-cultural dialogue: Pedagogy, desire, and absolution in the classroom. *Educational Theory, 49*(3), 299–316. https://doi.org/10.1111/j.1741-5446.1999.00299.x

Kawash, S. (1998). The homeless body. *Public Culture, 10*(2), 319. https://doi.org/10.1215/08992363-10-2-319

Kelly, C. (2016). *Disability politics and care: The challenge of direct funding*. University of British Columbia Press.

Kennedy, B. (2020, October 23). As standoff at "1492 Land Back Lane" heats up in Caledonia, land defenders say, "This is a moment for our people to say no." *Toronto Star*. https://www.thestar.com/news/gta/2020/10/23/as-standoff-at-1492-land-back-lane-heats-up-in-caledonia-land-defenders-say-this-is-a-moment-for-our-people-to-say-no.html

King, T. L. (2015). Interview with Dr. Tiffany Lethabo King. *Feral Feminisms, 4*, 64–86. https://feralfeminisms.com/wp-content/uploads/2015/12/ff_Interview-with-Dr.-Tiffany-Lethabo-King_issue4.pdf

The Kino-nda-niimi Collective. (2014). Idle no more: The winter we danced. In The Kino-nda-niimi Collective (Ed.), *The winter we danced* (pp. 21–6). Arbeiter Ring Publishing.

Kumashiro, K. (2000). Toward a theory of anti-oppressive education. *Review of Educational Research, 70*(1), 25–53. https://doi.org/10.3102/00346543070001025

Kvale, S., & Brinkmann, S. (2009). *InterViews: Learning the craft of qualitative research interviewing* (2nd ed.). Sage Publications.

Lavell-Harvard, M. D., & Brant, J. (2016). *Forever loved: Exposing the hidden crisis of missing and murdered Indigenous women and girls in Canada*. Demeter Press.

Lawrence, B. (2002). Colonization and Indigenous resistance in eastern Canada. In S. H. Razack. (Ed.), *Race, space and the law: Unmapping a white settler society* (pp. 21–46). Between the Lines.

Lawrence, B., & Dua, E. (2005). Decolonizing antiracism. *Social justice, 32*(4 (102)), 120–43.

Lensmire, T. J., McManimon, S. K., Dockter Tierney, J., Lee-Nichols, M. E., Casey, Z. A., Lensmire, A., & Davis, B. M. (2013). McIntosh as synecdoche:

How teacher education's focus on white privilege undermines antiracism. *Harvard Educational Review, 83*(3), 410–31. https://doi.org/10.17763/haer .83.3.35054h14l8230574

Leung, H. H. (2008). *Undercurrents: Queer culture and postcolonial Hong Kong.* University of British Columbia Press.

Linklater, R. (2014). *Decolonizing trauma work: Indigenous stories and strategies.* Fernwood Publishing.

Lorde, A. (1984). *Sister/outsider.* Crossing Press.

Lowman, E. B., & Barker, A. J. (2015). *Settler: Identity and colonialism in 21st century Canada.* Fernwood Publishing.

Mackey, E. (2002). *The house of difference: Cultural politics and national identity in Canada.* University of Toronto Press.

Matzner, A. (2015). *Stonewall riots.* GLBTQ Archive. http://www.glbtqarchive .com/ssh/stonewall_riots_S.pdf

Max, K. (2005). Anti-colonial research: Working as an ally with Aboriginal peoples. In G. S. Dei & G. S. Johal (Eds.), *Critical issues in anti-racist research methodologies* (pp. 79–94). Peter Lang.

Mbembe, A. (2003). Necropolitics. *Public Culture, 15*(1), 11–40. https://doi.org /10.1215/08992363-15-1-11

Mbembe, A. (2019). *Necropolitics.* Duke University Press.

McCready, L. T. (2004). Some challenges facing queer youth programs in urban high schools: Racial segregation and de-normalizing whiteness. *Journal of Gay & Lesbian Issues in Education, 1*(3), 37–51. DOI: 10.1300 /J367v01n03_05

McIntosh, P. (2010). White privilege and male privilege. In M. S. Kimmel & A. L. Ferber (Eds.), *Privilege: A reader* (2nd ed.) (pp. 13–26). Westview Press.

McNeil-Seymour, J. (2015). Cross-dancing as culturally restorative practice. In B. J. O'Neill, T. A. Swan, & N. J. Mule (Eds.), *LGBTQ People and Social Work: Intersectional Perspectives* (pp. 87–105). Canadian Scholars Press.

McNinch, J. (2008). Queer eye on straight youth: Homoerotics and racial violence in the narrative discourse of white settler masculinity. *Journal of LGBT Youth, 5*(2), 87–107. DOI: 10.1080/19361650802092499

Mikdashi, M. (2013). What is settler colonialism? (for Leo Delano Ames Jr.). *American Indian Culture and Research Journal, 37*(2), 23–34. https://doi.org /10.17953/aicr.37.2.c33g723731073714

Milar, K. (2011). The myth buster: Evelyn Hooker's groundbreaking research exploded the notion that homosexuality was a mental illness, ultimately removing it from the DSM. *Monitor on Psychology, 42*(2), 24. https://www .apa.org/monitor/2011/02/myth-buster

Miller, J. R. (1996). *Shingwauk's vision: A history of Native residential schools.* University of Toronto Press.

Million, D. (2013). *Therapeutic nations: Healing in the age of Indigenous human rights.* University of Arizona Press.

Monture-Angus, P. (1995). *Thunder in my soul: A Mohawk woman speaks.* Fernwood Publishers.

Monture-Angus, P. (1999). *Journeying forward: Dreaming First Nations independence.* Fernwood Publishers.

Morgensen, S. (2011a). The biopolitics of settler colonialism: Right here, right now. *Settler Colonial Studies, 1*(1), 52–76. DOI: 10.1080/2201473X.2011.10648801

Morgensen, S. (2011b). *The spaces between us: Queer settler colonialism and Indigenous decolonization.* University of Minnesota Press.

Morgensen, S. (2011c). Unsettling queer politics: What can non-Natives learn from two-spirit organizing. In Q. Driskill, C. Finley, B. J. Gilley, & S. L. Morgensen (Eds.), *Queer Indigenous studies: Critical interventions in theory, politics, and literature* (pp. 132–54). University of Arizona Press.

Morgensen, S. (2012). Queer settler colonialism in Canada and Israel: Articulating two-spirit and Palestinian queer critiques. *Settler Colonial Studies, 2*(2), 167–90. DOI: 10.1080/2201473X.2012.10648848

Muñoz, J. E. (1999). *Disidentifications: Queers of color and the performance of politics.* University of Minnesota Press.

Murdocca, C. (2009). From incarceration to restoration: National responsibility, gender and the production of cultural difference. *Social & Legal Studies, 18*(1), 23–45. https://doi.org/10.1177/0964663908100332

Nagy, R. L. (2013). The scope and bounds of transitional justice and the Canadian truth and reconciliation commission. *The International Journal of Transitional Justice, 7*(1), 52–73. https://doi.org/10.1093/ijtj/ijs034

Nash, C. J. (2005). Contesting identity: Politics of gays and lesbians in Toronto in the 1970s. *Gender, Place and Culture, 12*(1), 113–35. DOI: 10.1080/09663690500083115

Nash, C. J. (2006). Toronto's gay village (1969–1982): Plotting the politics of gay identity. *The Canadian Geographer, 50*(1), 1–16. https://doi.org/10.1111/j.0008-3658.2006.00123.x

Nash, C. J., & Bain, A. (2007). Pussies declawed: Unpacking the politics of a queer women's bathhouse raid. In K. Browne, J. Lim, & G. Brown (Eds.), *Geographies of sexualities: Theory, practices and politics* (pp. 159–67). Ashgate Publishing.

National Inquiry into Missing and Murdered Indigenous Women and Girls (Canada). (2019). *Reclaiming power and place: The final report of the National Inquiry into Missing and Murdered Indigenous Women and Girls.* National Inquiry into Missing and Murdered Indigenous Women and Girls.

Nguyen, V. (2010). *The republic of therapy: Triage and sovereignty in West Africa's time of AIDS.* Duke University Press.

Ontario HIV Treatment Network. (n.d.). *Men who have sex with men.* https://www.ohtn.on.ca/research-portals/priority-populations/men-who-have-sex-with-men/

O'Shane, P. (1995). The psychological impact of white colonialism on Aboriginal people. *Australasian Psychiatry, 3*(3), 149–53. https://journals .sagepub.com/doi/pdf/10.3109/10398569509080404?casa_token=kxGLme MWgAkAAAAA:RyqSla4yhWuYnG5WbyLirdLFOPqnHVjKT86HvQSkyi UOlJu6zfH-ZEfeJADp7VOS-I79kk6xStr5

Palacios, L. (2016). Challenging convictions: Indigenous and Black race-radical feminists theorizing the carceral state and abolitionist praxis in the United States and Canada. *Meridians, 15*(S1), 137–65. https://doi.org/10.1215 /15366936-8566133

Patel, S., Moussa, G., & Upadhyay, N. (2015). Complicities, connections, & struggles: Critical transnational feminist analysis of settler colonialism. *Feral Feminisms, 4*, 5–19. https://feralfeminisms.com/ complicities-connections-struggles/

Pateman, C. (2007). The settler contract. In C. Pateman & C. W. Mills, *Contract and Domination* (pp. 35–78). Polity Press.

Peterson, K. J., & Bricker-Jenkins, M. (1996). Lesbians and the health care system. *Journal of Gay & Lesbian Social Services, 5*(1), 33–48. DOI: 10.1300/ J041v05n01_03

Piepzna-Samarasinha, L. L. (2018). *Care work: Dreaming disability justice.* Arsenal Pulp Press.

Planned Parenthood. *Teens educating and confronting homophobia—t.e.a.c.h.* http://ppt.on.ca/volunteer/teens-educating-confronting-homophobia/

Pon, G. (2009). Cultural competency as new racism: An ontology of forgetting. *Journal of Progressive Human Services, 20*(1), 59–71, DOI: 10.1080/10428230902871173

Pon, G., Gosine, K., & Phillips, D. (2011). Immediate response: addressing anti-Native and anti-Black racism in child welfare. *International Journal of Child, Youth and Family Studies, 2*(3/4), 385–409. https://doi.org/10.18357/ ijcyfs23/420117763

Porter, R. (1999). The demise of Ongwehoweh and the ride of the Native Americans: Redressing the genocidal act of forcing American citizenship upon Indigenous peoples. *Harvard Black Letter Law Journal, 15*, 107–83. https://heinonline.org/HOL/P?h=hein.journals/hblj15&i=111

Povinelli, E. (2002). *The cunning of recognition: Indigenous alterities and the making of Australian multiculturalism.* Duke University Press.

Puar, J. (2007). *Terrorist assemblages: Homonationalism in queer times.* Duke University Press.

Putnam, R. D., Feldstein, L., & Cohen, D. J. (2004). Valley interfaith: The most dangerous thing we do is talk to our neighbors. In *Better together: Restoring the American community* (pp. 11–33). Simon and Schuster.

Ranlet, P. (2000). The British, the Indians, and smallpox: What actually happened at Fort Pitt in 1763? *Pennsylvania History: A Journal of Mid-Atlantic Studies, 67*(3), 427–41. https://www.jstor.org/stable/27774278

Rayside, D. M., & Lindquist, E. A. (1992). AIDS activism and the state in Canada. *Studies in Political Economy, 39*(1), 37–76. DOI: 10.1080/19187033. 1992.11675417

Razack, S. (1998). *Looking white people in the eye: Gender, race, and culture in courtrooms and classrooms*. University of Toronto Press.

Razack, S. (2002). When place becomes race. In S. H. Razack (Ed.), *Race, space, and the law: Unmapping a white settler society* (pp. 1–20). Between the Lines.

Razack, S. (2008). *Casting out: The eviction of Muslims from Western law and politics*. University of Toronto Press.

Razack, S. (2015). *Dying from improvement: Inquests and inquiries into Indigenous deaths in custody*. University of Toronto Press.

Razack, S., Smith, M., & Thobani, S. (2011). Introduction. In S. Razack, M. Smith, & S. Thobani (Eds.), *States of race: Critical race feminism for the 21st century* (pp. 1–22). Between the Lines.

Reagon, B. J. (1983) Coalition politics: Turning the century. In B. Smith (Ed.), *Home girls: A Black feminist anthology* (pp. 358–68). Kitchen Table: Women of Colour Press.

Recollet, K. (2013). For sisters. In D. H. Taylor (Ed.), *Me artsy: An exploration of contemporary Native arts* (pp. 103–4). Douglas & McIntyre.

Reddy, C. (2011). *Freedom with violence: Race, sexuality, and the US stat*. Duke University Press.

Regan, P. (2010). *Unsettling the settler within: Indian residential schools, truth telling, and reconciliation in Canada*. University of British Columbia Press.

Rifkin, M. (2013). Settler common sense. *Settler Colonial Studies, 3*(3/4), 322–40. DOI: 10.1080/2201473X.2013.810702

Ristock, J. L. (2001). Decentering heterosexuality: Responses of feminist counselors to abuse in lesbian relationships. *Women & Therapy, 23*(3), 59–72. DOI: 10.1300/J015v23n03_05

Rites Magazine for Lesbians and Gay Liberation. (1986). *Rights in Ontario?* (Vol. 3, No. 2). Canadian Gay and Lesbian Archives, Toronto, Ontario, Canada.

Rossiter, A. (2001). Innocence lost and suspicion found: Do we educate for or against social work? *Critical Social Work, 2*(1). https://ojs.uwindsor.ca/index.php/csw/article/view/5628

Sabzalian, L. (2019). The tensions between Indigenous sovereignty and multicultural citizenship education: Toward an anticolonial approach to civic education. *Theory & Research in Social Education, 47*(3), 311–46. DOI: 10.1080/00933104.2019.1639572

St. Denis, V. (2007). Aboriginal education and anti-racist education: Building alliances across cultural and racial identity. *Canadian Journal of Education/ Revue Canadienne De l'éducation, 30*(4), 1068–92. Retrieved from https://journals.sfu.ca/cje/index.php/cje-rce/article/view/2987

St. Denis, V. (2011). Silencing Aboriginal curricular content and perspectives through multiculturalism: "There are other children here." *Review of Education, Pedagogy, and Cultural Studies, 33*(4), 306–17. DOI: 10.1080/10714413.2011.597638

Schick, C. (2004). Disrupting binaries of self and other: Anti-homophobic pedagogies for student teachers. In J. McNinch & M. Cronin (Eds.), *I could not speak my heart: Education and social justice for gay and lesbian youth* (pp. 243–54). Canadian Plains Research Center/University of Regina.

Schick, C. (2014). White resentment in settler society. *Race Ethnicity and Education, 17*(1), 88–102. DOI: 10.1080/13613324.2012.733688

Schick, C., & McNinch, J. (2009). Introduction. In C. Schick & J. McNinch (Eds.), *"I thought Pocahontas was a movie": Perspectives on race/culture binaries in education and service professions* (pp. xi–xv). Canadian Plains Research Center Press.

Schick, C., & St. Denis, V. (2005). Troubling national discourses in anti-racist curricular planning. *Canadian Journal of Education / Revue Canadienne De L'éducation, 28*(3), 295–317. DOI:10.2307/4126472

Simon, R. I. (2005). Remembering otherwise: Civic life and the pedagogical promise of historical memory. In *The touch of the past: Remembrance, learning, and ethics* (pp. 1–13). Palgrave Macmillan.

Simon, R. I. (2013). Towards a hopeful practice of worrying: The problematics of listening and the educative responsibilities of the IRSTRC. In P. Wakeham & J. Henderson (Eds.), *Reconciling Canada: Historical injustices and the contemporary culture of redress* (pp. 129–42). University of Toronto Press.

Simpson, J. S., James, C. E., & Mack, J. (2011). Multiculturalism, colonialism, and racialization: Conceptual starting points. *The Review of Education, Pedagogy, and Critical Studies, 33*(4), 285–305. DOI: 10.1080/10714413.2011.597637

Skills for Solidarity. (2014, July 31). *About the program.* Skills for Solidarity. http://www.leadnow.ca/skills-for-solidarity/

Smith, L. T. (1999). *Decolonizing methodologies: Research and Indigenous peoples.* St. Martin's Press.

Smith, L. T. (2012). Foreword. In *Decolonizing methodologies: Research and Indigenous peoples* (2nd ed., pp. ix–xv). Zed Books.

Srivastava, S. (2005). "You're calling me a racist?" The moral and emotional regulation of antiracism and feminism. *Signs, 31*(1), 29–62. https://doi.org/10.1086/432738

Srivastava, S., & Francis, M. (2006). The problem of authentic experience: Storytelling in anti-racist and anti-homophobic education. *Critical Sociology, 32*(2–3), 275–307. https://doi.org/10.1163/156916306777835330

Strega, S., & Sohki Aski Esquao [Carriere, J]. (2009). Introduction. In S. Strega & Sohki Aski Esquao [J. Carriere] (Eds.), *Walking this path together: Anti-racist and anti-oppressive child welfare practice* (pp. 15–28). Fernwood Publishing.

Talaga, T. (2017). *Seven fallen feathers: Racism, death, and hard truths in a northern city.* House of Anansi.

Thatcher, R. (2004). *Fighting firewater fictions: Moving beyond the disease model of alcoholism in First Nations.* University of Toronto Press.

Thobani, S. (2007). *Exalted subjects: Studies in the making of race and nation in Canada.* University of Toronto Press.

Tuck, E., & Yang, K. W. (2012). Decolonization is not a metaphor. *Decolonization: Indigeneity, Education, and Society, 1*(1), 1–40.

Vaughan, M. (1991). *Curing their ills: Colonial power and African illness.* Stanford University Press.

Vowel, C. (2016). *Indigenous writes: A guide to First Nations, Métis, and Inuit issues in Canada.* Portage & Main Press.

Walcott, R. (2011). Disgraceful: Intellectual dishonesty, white anxieties, and multicultural critique thirty-six years later. In M. Chazan, L. Helps, A. Stanley, & S. Thakkar (Eds.), *Home and native land: Unsettling multiculturalism in Canada* (pp. 15-30). Between the Lines.

Walcott, R. (2017). Black Lives Matter, police, and pride: Toronto activists spark a movement. *The Conversation.* https://the conversation.com/black-lives-matter-police-and-pride-toronto-activists -spark-a-movement-79089

Waldorf, S. (2012). *Moving beyond cultural inclusion towards a curriculum of settler colonial responsibility: A teacher education curriculum analysis* [Unpublished master's thesis]. University of Toronto.

Walia, H. (2013). *Undoing border imperialism.* AK Press.

Ward, J. (2015). *Not gay: Sex between straight white men.* New York University Press.

Waterfall, B. (2002). Native people and the social work profession: A critical exploration of colonizing problematics and the development of decolonized thought. *Journal of Educational Thought, 36*(2), 149–66. http://www.jstor.org/stable/23767599

Willinsky, J. (1998). The educational mission. In *Learning to divide the world: Education at empire's end* (pp. 89–114). University of Minnesota Press.

Wilson, A. (1996). How we find ourselves: Identity development and two-spirit people. *Harvard Educational Review, 66*(2), 303–18. https://doi.org/10.17763/haer.66.2.n551658577h927h4

Wilson, A. (2008). N'tacinowin inna nah': Our coming in stories. *Canadian Woman Studies, 26*(3), 193–9.

Wolfe, P. (2006). Settler colonialism and the elimination of the Native. *Journal of Genocide Research, 8*(4), 387–409. DOI: 10.1080/14623520601056240

Wolfe, P. (2013.) Recuperating binarism: a heretical introduction. *Settler Colonial Studies, 3*(3–4), 257–79, DOI: 10.1080/2201473X.2013.830587

Woolford, A. (2013). Nodal repair and networks of destruction: Residential schools, colonial genocide and redress in Canada. *Settler Colonial Studies, 3*(1), 61–77. DOI: 10.1080/18380743.2013.761936

Wotherspoon, T. (2009). Historical and organizational dimensions of Canadian education. In *The sociology of education in Canada: Critical perspectives* (pp. 54–77). Oxford University Press Canada.

Yee, J. Y., & Dumbrill, G. (2003). Whiteout: Looking for race in Canadian social work practice. In A. Al-Krenawi & J. R. Graham (Eds.), *Multicultural social work in Canada* (pp. 98–121). Oxford University Press.

Young, R. M., & Meyer, I. H. (2005). The trouble with "MSM" and "WSW": Erasure of the sexual-minority person in public health discourse. *American Journal of Public Health, 95*(7), 1144–9. https://doi.org/10.2105/AJPH.2004.046714

Index